A Whisper of Lace

Gillian Cross

A Whisper of Lace

Oxford University Press 1981

Oxford   New York   Toronto   Melbourne

Oxford University Press, Walton Street, Oxford OX2 6DP

London Glasgow New York Toronto
Delhi Bombay Calcutta Madras Karachi
Kuala Lumpur Singapore Hong Kong Tokyo
Nairobi Dar es Salaam Cape Town Salisbury
Melbourne Wellington

and associate companies in
Beirut Berlin Ibadan Mexico City

British Library Cataloguing in Publication Data
Cross, Gillian
A whisper of lace.
I. Title
823'.9'1J   80-41466
ISBN 0-19-271447-3

Photoset in Great Britain by
Rowland Phototypesetting Limited
Bury St Edmunds, Suffolk
and printed by Biddles Ltd,
Guildford, Surrey

Prologue

Y OU'LL get us all hanged!' The old man's voice grated
scornfully, no louder than a whisper, as he bent over the map,
his grey hair hanging lank round his gaunt face. 'Cam-handed
scheme! Us'll swing for certain.' He snatched up his glass of
wine and gulped it down.

The man in the black coat said nothing. His face was expressionless. But the man in the brown coat smiled unpleasantly.

'If you *don't* do as I say, Zachary, you'll land on the
gallows for sure, won't you?' He looked down at his fingernails.
'If I give the information I have about you to the proper
authorities.'

The old man spat into a corner, his bony face stubborn. But
his hand clenched more tightly round his glass.

'Philippe!' called the man in brown. He waved an arm at the
boy who shuffled through from the front of the inn. 'Encore du
vin pour Monsieur.' He watched silently as the boy brought
another bottle of wine and filled Zachary's glass. Then he
leaned forward in a businesslike way.

'So. We are agreed?'

Zachary nodded, his mouth twisting wryly, and the man in
brown pulled the map closer.

'The first landing will be made – here.' His finger moved up
the line of the canal and stabbed at the blob which said *Exeter*.
'And if that one is successful, perhaps another one – here.'
Another stab, further east.

The three heads drew together over the map as they
discussed the plan in low voices. The loudest sound in the
dirty, bare little room was the rasp of Zachary's whisper.

5

After a few moments the old man straightened, frowning.

'The worst part be still to settle,' he whispered harshly. 'Who's to meet the cargo? Gentlemen and ladies, it should be. *I'll* never find anyone to fool the officers. And if they fail, we're all done.'

'I have thought of that,' the man in brown said calmly. He snapped his fingers and, still without speaking, his companion produced pen, ink and paper. 'I shall give you a letter to deliver to someone in London. He is a trifle – inexperienced – but I think you'll find that when he has read my letter he will do what you tell him and take care of that side of the matter.' Spreading the paper on top of the map, he picked up the pen and dipped it into the ink. Then, pausing, he transferred the pen from his right hand to his left and began to shape the letters, slowly and awkwardly, the quill scratching and sputtering. The other two watched him as he signed the letter, *James Prior*, finishing with an emphatic dot. Folding it up, he dropped a blob of sealing wax on the join, blew it dry and wrote the direction on the front, his lips curling slightly as if something amused him. The man in black leaned forward to peer over his shoulder and tensed suddenly.

'Is that wise?' he murmured.

'Very wise,' the writer said curtly. 'Here, Zachary.'

The old man took the letter between his thumb and forefinger and glanced down at the address.

To Mr Francis Merrowby at 57a Duke Street, London.

'You will take it yourself,' said the man in brown crisply, 'and if he agrees – *when* he agrees – you will get my letter back and burn it before you tell him our plans. You cross to England tonight?'

'With the tide.'

'So. Bon voyage.'

The old man looked at him sardonically. ''Twill be none the better for thy part in it,' he muttered under his breath. Then he slid out of the room. The man in the black coat sat down abruptly at the table.

'Is it wise?' he murmured again. 'To involve Mr Francis Merrowby? I think you take too much of a risk, sir.'

6

'No risk at all,' the other man said shortly. 'Whether we succeed or fail, I gain by involving Francis.'

And he began to laugh, softly and chillingly.

Chapter 1

*T*HE post-chaise crunched up the sloping gravel drive, a swaying black shadow in the gathering darkness. Swinging the horses round in front of the Hall, the postilion heaved on the reins and muttered to the animals as they paced to a halt. There was only a brief pause. A tall, great-coated figure climbed from inside and flung a coin to the postilion who caught it neatly. Then, at a twitch of the reins, the horses wheeled round and trotted back down the tree-lined drive.

The man who was left alone stood staring up at the building in front of him. Bland and pale in the moonlight, its massive façade stretched elegantly wide. Bending to pick up his travelling bag, he climbed the steps to the front door and his knock thudded dully in the silence.

When the heavy door swung open, the light from inside sent his long shadow pouring jaggedly down the steps behind him and lit up his narrow, humorous face. In the brightness, his fair, curly hair gleamed almost white, its neatly tied tail falling over his collar at the back. He stepped inside and the door clicked shut, leaving the spacious circular forecourt empty and dark.

He had not observed the sharp eyes watching him from high under the roof, nor seen the attentive face peering out of the window.

'Someone's come,' Betty said, without turning round. There was a grunt from the shadows behind her.

'Be nothing to us.' The slumped figure in the corner of the room laughed bitterly. 'Bain't come to visit us. Stuck away up here.'

9

Betty turned quickly from the window and looked across the room at her aunt. The nurse was huddled in the rocking-chair by the fire, staring gloomily at the flames which made the only light in the room. The red glow shadowed every wrinkle in her grey, exhausted face and flickered over her hunched body. She looked like a battered marionette, flung carelessly in a heap.

'They never come up here,' her voice grumbled on. 'Not to see us as rocked and dandled 'em all those years. Leave us off with their petticoats they do.' A tear ran erratically down a groove in her cheek.

'Aunt –' Betty took a step forward into the room. 'Proper tired, aren't 'ee?'

'Mustn't call me aunt.' The old woman wagged a shaky finger at her. 'Told 'ee afore. I be nurse here. Nurse, God help me.'

Betty walked briskly across the room and took her aunt's elbow. 'Come on. Come to bed. Thee'll do no good here.'

'The babby,' the nurse said muzzily. 'Got to stay awake. Got to take the babby to her la'ship soon. To be fed.' She snorted sleepily. 'Should've had a wet nurse, like her did for the others. Newfangled, crack-pated notion of Sir Horatio's! He –'

'Come on. Bed.' Her thin arms straining, Betty heaved the old woman to her feet. 'I can take the babby down. 'Course I can.' She took her aunt's weight on her shoulder and, with the other hand, she fished a bottle out of the rocking-chair. Best to hide it. Just in case.

Still mumbling, the old woman staggered across the room, leaning heavily on her niece, as if every step were a weariness to her. Betty piloted her through the bedroom door and let her fall across the bed. Almost immediately, the nurse began to snore softly. The girl lifted the frail legs on to the bed and slipped her aunt's shoes from her twisted feet.

'Too much for 'ee,' she said softly. 'Nigh on fifty and still tending babbies?' With protective gentleness, she pulled a blanket over the nurse's body.

As she stepped back into the dark nursery, her nose

10

twitched at an unfamiliar smell. A faint scent of lavender water mingled with the smoke from the fire. There was someone else in the room. Peering, Betty made out a dark shape crouched in front of the hearth.

'Sitting in the dark, nurse?' said a voice. From the fireplace yellow light swelled at the tip of a newly lit candle and the figure straightened, lifting it to brighten the room. 'I came to tell you – oh.' The voice died away and the speaker looked doubtfully at Betty.

Betty looked back, bobbing a curtsey as she stared. She knew who it was well enough. Seen them all she had, peering from her high window. But never so dressed up as this. All pale silk and lace ruffles – good Honiton lace, Betty noted, with a professional eye. And hair piled high and powdered white. Still, it was Miss Selina all right. There was no mistaking those over-heated brown eyes, that mobile mouth and the unfashionable flush on her cheeks.

Selina's emphatic eyebrows arched questioningly. 'I thought you were the nurse.'

'The rocker, miss.' Betty bobbed another curtsey. ''Lisbeth Pinney. Help with the babby.'

The brown eyes scanned her. Betty knew what they were seeing. A scrawny twelve-year-old with a dirty apron and strands of greasy hair across her forehead. Resisting an urge to straighten her cap, she held her head higher. 'Been here a fortnight, miss.'

'Oh? I don't think I've seen you.'

'Haven't been up here, have 'ee?' Unwarily, Betty let a note of bitterness creep into her voice and the older girl's eyes glittered. But with interest, not outrage. All she said, however, was, 'Well, I'm here now. I've come to see nurse. Where is she?'

Automatically, Betty took a step backwards to shield the bedroom door. 'Her's asleep. Can't see her now.'

'*Asleep*? At five in the evening?'

'Broken nights,' Betty said quickly. 'There's always broken nights with a new babby. 'Tes why I be come. To help her out.'

'Well –' an arm reached out to jam the candle into the candlestick on the mantelpiece – 'when she wakes, you may tell her that my brother, Mr Francis Merrowby, has come visiting. I came up specially to tell her, because I knew she would like to hear.' Selina turned away, but as she did so a restless murmur came from the cradle in the corner. Then a louder murmur. Selina turned back. 'He sounds hungry. Lady Merrowby is in the drawing-room. She's finished her dinner. Will you bring the baby down if nurse is asleep?'

Betty nodded and Selina swirled across to the door and crossed the landing, her silk slippers making no sound on the bare boards. Ignoring the baby's growing yells, Betty went to the door and watched curiously as the slender green figure billowed down the stairs.

'Proper dressed up,' she murmured aloud. 'Not like the last time I saw 'ee.' In her mind she could still picture the white heap in the grass where the hooped petticoat lay discarded. She could see the big oak tree jerking its branches as Selina scrambled up in her print gown. And those brown eyes, alive and excited, peering out between the twigs to keep watch in case anyone sneaked up and caught her at it. Miss Selina was no ordinary young lady. Not for all her silk and lace.

The baby would not be ignored any longer. It was yelling itself into a frenzy, its wrinkled face turning purple. Betty scooped the squirming bundle out of the cradle. 'Hush up, now. Got to find that drawing-room of theirn. Ssh!'

Rocking the child against her shoulder to quiet it, she went determinedly on her way. The bedroom floor was familiar enough. Every night she took the baby down to Lady Merrowby's chamber to be fed. And she knew the way down the back stairs to the kitchen. But the front, the main part of the house, was strange territory, seen only in surreptitious peeps over the banisters. Leaving the cosy, cluttered darkness of the nursery behind her, she went steadily down the stairs.

The great marble entrance hall was huge and chilly, and she shivered slightly, cuddling the murmuring baby to her. Like a cave it was down here. Smooth walls loomed up, high as a church, and, from the walls, the stiff faces in the portraits stared down disapprovingly. *Interloper. Cottage girl.* She could almost hear their voices. *Grubby feet in our grand hall.*

Betty tossed her head. Stubborn enough for three, her mother used to call her. Not allowing herself to be frightened, she gazed round, an obstinate, upright little figure on the edge of the great sea of shiny floor. All about her were heavy, closed doors. Since the baby was quiet, no one came to ask her business and for a moment she stared helplessly at the doors. Then, from behind one of them, she caught a murmur of voices. Timidly she knocked. There was no answer. Turning the handle, she pushed the door open.

At once, she turned scarlet with embarrassment. It was the wrong room. From around the smooth expanse of a big mahogany table, faces turned to stare at her. Men's faces. There was Sir Horatio, his face puffy and foppish under a powdered wig. And the bony old tutor in his rusty black. But the eyes that caught hers were green and mocking, set in an elegant, ironic face. That face she had seen only once, on the doorstep. Mr Francis Merrowby.

'Well, girl?' Sir Horatio's drawl was irritated. 'What brings you bursting in here?'

'B-beg pardon, sir.' Her confusion made her stammer. ''Tes the babby. To be fed.'

'God's death,' murmured Francis, amused, '*we're* no use to you, girl.'

Round the table, the faces split into grins, and Sir Horatio tittered. But, at Francis's side, a smaller figure stood up quietly and limped across towards Betty.

'My mother's in the drawing-room. I'll show you.'

'Thankee, Master Daniel.' Still embarrassed, Betty gazed not at his face but at the heavy boot he dragged on his left foot. Poor little soul. Seen him she had, as well, from her window. Limping about as if he didn't know what to do with himself. As she followed him out of the room, she heard Sir Horatio say, needlessly loud, 'That's the trouble with these cottage girls. No idea of how to behave in a gentleman's house.'

Silly creature, she thought furiously. Painted and powdered like a woman.

Daniel pulled the door to behind them. 'It's a good idea to knock,' he said gently. 'Before you come in.'

Betty coloured again. 'And if no one hears? I'm to stand all night in the hall with the babby screaming?'

Her annoyance made her vehement and Daniel blinked, surprised. He opened his mouth to reply and then drew back, like a snail that has been touched and curls into its shell. All he said was, 'This is the drawing-room.'

Betty nodded her thanks, almost rudely, as she knocked, and watched him hobble back to the dining-room. Feeble as well as lame, she thought sharply. A button short in his wits, maybe.

'Come in.' It was Lady Merrowby's voice. She sat at a little table, the spirit lamp and the silver tea-kettle in front of her. Her whole body was rigid. Stiff corsets, stiff powdered hair, stiff brocade skirts. But her face, held as stiffly as everything else, was incongruous, the round, rosy face of a Devon countrywoman. Beside her, Selina, who lounged on the sofa feeding titbits to a little dog, was frail and slender.

'Oh. The baby.' The stiff expression did not alter, but Lady Merrowby stood up at once. 'I'll feed him in the closet. Bring him through.'

Betty followed her into the little room and stood awkwardly for a moment. Lady Merrowby was motionless on a chair and the baby was starting to cry again.

'Come on, girl,' Lady Merrowby said impatiently, and Betty realized what she was meant to do. Fumbling one-handed, she unfastened the front of Lady Merrowby's bodice and un-did the tight lacing of the stays beneath. Almost eagerly, Lady Merrowby reached out for the baby and, as it began to suck, flapped a hand.

'Well, off you go till I'm ready. You know he won't feed properly if there's anyone to distract him.'

Betty stepped back into the drawing-room, closing the closet door after her. As she turned, she saw Selina stretch inelegantly, pulling the silk of her bodice into tight wrinkles. Her mouth stretched wide into a yawn.

Seeing Betty, she smiled. 'Another exciting evening in the home of Sir Horatio Merrowby,' she murmured sarcastically.

'Life! Action! Drama!'

'Yes, miss,' Betty said obediently. But she could not help herself. An answering grin spread across her face.

'You see it too?' Selina said mockingly. 'The robbers? The highwaymen? The bloodthirsty corsairs?'

Betty knew what Aunt Annie would say. Not her place to comment. She mastered her features. '''Tes all very nice, miss,' she said meekly.

'Nice?' Selina's eyebrows arched. *'Nice?'* She flourished a hand round the room with its uncomfortable little chairs and its arabesques of white plaster on pale blue walls. In the pictures, elegant shepherdesses stood frozen in unreal landscapes, and in the corner cabinet two china squirrels faced each other, their tails pricked and their heads bent to nibble nuts they would never taste. 'Do you know what I'd like to do to this nice, proper room? I'd like to take a huge hammer and smash it to pieces. *Then* we'd see some excitement.' Her fist came down hard on the arm of the sofa.

'''Tes boring, I guess,' Betty said incautiously, 'for a young lady like yourself.'

'Like me?' Selina leaned forward suddenly almost feverishly alert. 'What do you mean, like me? I am exquisite, refined, elegant.' She flourished a lace-encircled arm. 'The very young lady to grace a room like this.' But her face was teasing, as if she were eager for contradiction, and Betty was surprised into imprudence.

'Seen 'ee, I have. Climbing the oak tree.'

'Oh.' For a moment Selina was startled into silence, staring quizzically at her. Then she gave a wry smile. 'Climbing trees? No, you are mistaken. Young ladies don't climb trees. Whatever would my father and mother say?'

Betty imagined the powdered, overdressed Sir Horatio and the stiff Lady Merrowby. 'No, miss,' she murmured quickly. 'Like you said, 'twas a mistake.'

But Selina was watching her conspiratorially, with a hectic gaiety that frightened Betty. It was all right for young ladies to play their games. They had no place to lose. But it would not do for a cottage girl to mix in it.

'I'll wait outside, miss. Till her la'ship's done.' Evading those eager eyes, she slid out into the hall and waited, sensibly still and quiet, until Lady Merrowby called her.

When she went back to the nursery, the candle had blown out and the fire had burned low. The room was chilly and shadowed. Setting the baby in its crib, Betty made up the fire, rattling the irons against the scuttle. As the flames leaped up, she seemed to see the shapes of the Merrowby family dancing across the black lumps of coal. Sir Horatio, peevish and effeminate. Lady Merrowby, corseted as stiff as a wooden doll. And the little cripple boy, dragging his boot. But the two which leaped highest and flickered fastest were the two which had caught her fancy. One dark and one fair. Selina, with her nervous eagerness and Francis with his cool, mocking face. Selina and Francis. Both full of an energy that leaped as restless and hungry as the flames. But hungry for what?

Curling up on the window-seat, Betty tried to doze, catching at a little sleep before she had to wake again. But the baby was colicky and restless, even after it had been taken down to Lady Merrowby's bedroom for its night feed, and Betty spent the night midway between sleep and waking, mesmerized by the tall shadows which danced round the nursery fire.

Towards morning, her aunt woke. She shuffled out of the bedroom, bleary and still exhausted, rubbing her eyes.

'How did 'ee make out?' she muttered.

Betty shrugged sleepily. 'Well enough. But I be proper lagged out.'

'No one axed for me?'

'No one. Oh –' Suddenly, Betty remembered. 'Miss Selina came up. To tell 'ee as 'twas Mr Francis came in the postchay. All alone.' She looked up curiously at her aunt. 'A strange one, that. He be the eldest?' She could imagine him as an elegant Sir Francis.

'Him?' The nurse grimaced. ''Twould be better, happen. He've got the family spirit. The living spit of old Sir James, his granfer, he be. Careless as a lord, and with a tongue to charm an ogre. "Nurse," he'd say to me, when he was no more'n six, "Nurse, I'm a bad boy. Torn my stockings bird's-nesting. You'll have to whip me." And all with a smile so sweet as a sun-beam.'

'But he's *not* the heir?'

'The heir?' The nurse spat the words out. 'No, the heir's the one as stood at the bottom of the tree, keeping his own stockings clean. Urging Francis up and waiting to take the eggs for hisself. That's Mr George. Gets it from his other granfer, Mr Turner, Lady Merrowby's father, as made a fortune in the cloth trade and kept it tight in his hand. George was always a one for getting and having and keeping, with no trouble to hisself. Could always talk hisself into Sir Horatio's good graces, too. But *I* know.' She nodded sagely. 'A nurse sees. When he went off to foreign parts, atravelling to see the ruins, I near cheered for joy. But Francis –' her face softened – 'I cried a bucketful when he went to live in London. 'Twas like losing one of my own.'

'Well, he's back,' Betty said. 'And couldn't wait, by the look of 'en. Coming in the dark like that, when dinner was done. And not even a manservant with 'en.'

'Not like him to be in a rush.' The old nurse looked thoughtful as she raised a clawlike hand to straighten her cap. 'He was always a one for lolloping about as if tomorrow would do.' She brooded, her face sharp. 'What's he after then, to travel so fast? What've he come for?'

Chapter 2

DANIEL, sitting in the breakfast-room the next morning, asked himself the same question. The sunlight filtered through the window on to the froth of his cup of chocolate and he looked across it at Francis, who was lounging peacefully in his chair. He had come in such a rush last night, travelling post and alone, and then – nothing. No startling news, no urgent demands. He had sat calmly in the drawing-room, teasing Selina and regaling Sir Horatio with the latest trivial gossip from London.

Shifting his withered leg into a more comfortable position, Dan frowned slightly, and Francis glanced up at him.

'Yes? Is there something bothering you, little brother?'

Dan shook his head silently and sipped his chocolate, but Francis was not so easily satisfied.

'I know that look,' he said mockingly. 'That frown as if you were a philosopher pondering the world's problems. What are you thinking?'

'I was wondering,' said Dan awkwardly, reaching for a piece of toast, 'what made you come so suddenly last night. It's nearly a year since we saw you.'

'Oh, *Daniel!*' Francis's face crinkled reproachfully. 'I am a devoted son. An adoring brother. I came to see my family, of course.'

With a nod, Dan began to spread butter on his toast, thinking his own thoughts, but Francis was enjoying himself. 'I've been away too long,' he said, mockingly grave. 'Look at you. Turned twelve, and grown a good two inches. And Sal! I would hardly have known her.'

'Sal?' said Dan stupidly. As if he did not understand.

'Yes, Sal. Miss Merrowby. Our elegant sister Selina. She has grown as cool and proper as a wax doll. Last time I saw her she was a positive romp. Why, I remember seeing you both rampage through the gardens. She was yelling something about blood and gunpowder and you were waving a long stick. What was it? Pirates?'

'Something like that,' Dan said in a gruff voice. It still hurt him to realize how much things had changed. But Francis pursued the subject.

'It was like a play to see you limping along at high speed to keep up with her. And yet now – I could swear she had never done anything but sit in the schoolroom doing fancy-work. What has happened to her?'

'It was Father.' Dan kept his voice steady. 'Before the baby was born, Mother took to her bed and Father expected Sal to accompany him and act as hostess. To take Mother's place. I think it was the first time he had ever looked at Sal properly. There was a terrible row and he said that she was a hoyden, and would never make a good marriage. So he gave – orders.'

'*Dear* Father,' murmured Francis. 'So Sal is to make a good marriage, is she? To wipe out the blot on the family tree that Father made when he married a cloth merchant's daughter.'

'Mother's not a blot,' Dan said stoutly. 'And there was nothing wrong with Grandfather Turner.'

'Nothing but a greed for money and a disregard for other people.' Francis smiled absently. 'And that is not what Father disapproves of. He hates only the label of merchant. Otherwise he would have us all as dull and respectable. And Sally is fitting into the mould, is she? Losing all her devil-may-care spirit?'

His voice was still light, but Dan, glancing up suddenly, noticed his eyes. They were narrowed and calculating. And they flicked away from meeting Dan's.

'I – don't know,' Dan said slowly. 'She certainly wouldn't dare play pirates any more. But I'm not sure how she feels.'

'Not sure how who feels?' came a voice from the door. Selina sailed across the room and sat down at the table. 'What makes you both so solemn?'

Dan blushed, but Francis was completely unruffled. He swallowed his last piece of toast and wiped his fingers on a napkin before he answered. 'We are discussing the reasons for my unexpected visit. Dan cannot believe that it was prompted by sheer family affection.'

'And you're saying that it was?' Selina arched her eyebrows delicately. '*That's* why you've come?'

'Now let me see.' Francis held up his fingers, ticking off the members of the family. 'Mother. Mother knows why I've come. She thinks I've come to see this new brother she has so startlingly provided. And Father. He knows too, but he's certain that I've come to ask for money.'

'And you haven't?' Selina's eyes widened in amused disbelief.

'Money never comes amiss. Maybe I shall make a small request in a day or two, since Father expects it. And Dan.' The green eyes swivelled round and scanned Daniel's face. 'No, he is not so easy to read. He will have to tell us. Why have I come, Dan?'

'Perhaps,' Dan said quietly, 'you haven't come *for* something. Perhaps you were hurrying away *from* something.'

'Oh, a most subtle idea,' Francis said delightedly. 'What could it be, I wonder?' With a teasing smile, he looked from one to the other. 'Shall I tell you a story?'

'Why not?' said Selina. She was pouring her chocolate and buttering her toast and Francis did not start at once. He waited until she was looking at him and then, fixing his eyes on hers, he began softly.

'Well now, a young man I know slightly – a foolish young man, far too rich for his own good – happened to be driving across Blackheath some months ago. Being a foolish young man, he travelled with only one servant, and quite unarmed.' Francis shook his fair curls. '*So* foolish.'

'And what happened?' Selina was absorbed.

'What he should have expected, of course.' Francis smiled slightly and tapped a finger on the table. 'It was dark.

Shadows everywhere. And suddenly, out of the shadows, rode a masked figure, waving a pistol. Breathing *terrible* threats. Most distressing to a foolish young man.' Without moving his eyes from Selina's face, he picked up his cup and drained it.

'And?' she said excitedly, her elbows on the table and her chin cupped in her hands.

'And, of course, the young man handed over his money and his watch. *Not* an elegant watch, I fear. The very rich do not always have good taste. The masked figure bowed gracefully and rode off into the night. A neat operation. But –'

'But?' Selina breathed.

'But unfortunately, several weeks later, the highwayman received a letter. Describing the incident on Blackheath. And describing his horse.' Francis put his cup down on the saucer with a clatter. 'A fine chestnut, with three white stockings.'

'Francis! Not –' Selina's hand clenched on her piece of toast and Dan saw it break into spiky crumbs.

'That's a hanging matter,' he interrupted flatly.

'Ah, Daniel. Still there?' Francis turned to him. 'Of course it is. Most distressing for the poor highwayman, if they catch him.' He stood up languidly.

'And *that's* why you've come?' murmured Selina.

'Dear Sal! How could you think it?' Francis smiled ironically. 'I see you are still a bloodthirsty romantic after all. No, I came to see you, of course. It is such a pleasure to have a beautiful, ladylike sister.' For an instant he looked at her gravely while she blushed and lowered her eyes. 'Now I am going to walk down by the lake. To enjoy this delightful sunshine.'

As he left the room, Selina sat up straighter and poured herself another cup of chocolate. 'I had forgotten what a tease Francis is,' she said briskly. But the chocolate jug wavered in her hand and Dan saw the printed cotton of her bodice pull tight as she breathed hard. He felt curiously uneasy, as though he should warn her against something.

'Sal –'

'Yes?' Her eyes were cool and expressionless as she looked up.

'Oh. Nothing.' What could he say, after all? 'I must go to my lesson now. Mr Heron will be waiting.'

He limped away as calmly as he could, but as he climbed the stairs and walked along the landing to the library he could still see Francis's calculating green eyes and Selina's excited brown ones. And he was oddly disturbed. Pushing open the library door, he greeted Mr Heron absentmindedly and the old tutor, stooped over the table at the far end of the long library, gave him a careful glance. But he did not say anything. Instead, he opened, with lovingly gentle hands, the battered leather cover of the *Aeneid*.

'I shall read, Daniel,' he said gravely, 'and then you can translate. You have prepared?' Dan gave a vague nod. 'Good. Now listen.'

Sitting down, Dan looked out of the window, across the terraced gardens and over the grassy slope which led down to the lake. He could see Francis, a slender figure in grey, pacing slowly along the near shore, and he watched the figure and its inverted reflection as Mr Heron's voice rolled across the table, savouring the sound of the words.

> '. . . . sate sanguine divum
> Tros Anchisiade, facilis descensus Averno:
> noctes atque dies patet atri ianua Ditis;
> sed revocare gradum superasque evadere ad auras,
> hoc opus, hic labor est . . . .'

At last the voice stopped. 'Now you,' Mr Heron said.

Dan took up the book and began on his prepared translation, the words coming back to him as he read the Latin on the page. 'In these words he prayed and placed his hands on the altar, and while he prayed thus –'

Out of the corner of his eye, he caught a pale flutter on the green of the grass and involuntarily he looked sideways and his voice faltered. Selina was running down the slope towards the lake.

'The prophetess spoke,' prompted Mr Heron mildly. 'Go on, Daniel.'

22

'Er – oh yes. She spoke: Seed of the divine blood, Trojan Anchises – no, I mean –'

'Trojan *son* of Anchises.' Mr Heron put a gentle hand on his arm. 'Is something the matter, Daniel?'

'No. No, of course not. I'm sorry.' Dan went on, more attentively, but still with half an eye watching out of the window. 'Trojan son of Anchises, the descent to Hell is easy.' Now Selina had reached the bottom of the slope, and Francis was standing waiting for her. 'Night and day, the door of black Dis stands open.'

Before Selina reached him, Francis had begun to walk away slowly, round the edge of the lake, and she hurried after him until she had caught up.

'But to call back – to retrace the step,' Dan gabbled, 'and to escape to the upper air, that is the task, that is the labour.' As his lips moved, he was thinking that Francis had known. He had known that Selina would go down to the lake to meet him.

'Stop for a moment,' Mr Heron said. 'Now, in that half line you have just translated, there is an interesting grammatical oddity.'

Dan wrenched his eyes away from the window and tried to concentrate. Normally he would have been interested. He loved the precision of the Latin, the careful unravelling of its intricacies. His lessons with Mr Heron were usually the brightest part of the day. Especially since Selina had changed and grown so – His eyes slid sideways again. The two figures had disappeared among the trees at the side of the lake, but he could still see their reflections in the smooth, grey sheet of water. They were walking very close and their heads were together.

Suddenly Mr Heron shut the book with a loud smack and Dan looked at him, startled. The old tutor's beaky face was wistful.

'I can see we shall do no good like this today,' he said regretfully. 'I must set you a passage to translate into Latin. Find me something.'

Apologetically, Dan got to his feet, opened the diamond-paned door of the nearest bookcase and, without thinking, stretched out a hand towards the row of ribbed leather spines. His finger closed around a familiar volume and, by the time he realized what he had taken, it was too late. Mr Heron had opened the book, smiling quizzically.

'What have we here? *A General History of the Robberies and Murders of the Most Notorious Pirates*? Well, it will enlarge your vocabulary, I have no doubt. You must remember, of course, that *pirata* – a pirate – is of the feminine form, but the masculine gender. Now –'

He began to leaf through, and the book fell open automatically. As Dan had known it would. As it always did. At the account of Blackbeard, that giant pirate who wore three pairs of pistols and stuck lighted matches under his hat. For a moment, Dan could hardly breathe. For a whole year, Selina had been Blackbeard and he had been Henry Morgan. Adventuring up and down the house and through the park, his withered leg forgotten in the hectic excitement of their exploits.

Mr Heron's fingers turned a page and there it was. The underlined passage. The passage Dan knew by heart, where Blackbeard shot his crewman, Israel Hands, in the knee while they sat at table. Dan's ears tingled as if he could still hear Selina's chilling shout, relishing the words. *'Why, damn you, if I did not now and then kill one of you, you would forget who I am!'*

'This seems to be a favourite passage,' said Mr Heron, disapproving because the book was defaced. 'Someone has underlined it, I see. Such curious brown ink, too. Translate, if you will, from here – to here.' He indicated the places and then stood up. 'And perhaps it would be as well if you sat with your back to the window?'

Dan shifted his seat and looked up remorsefully. 'I'm sorry, sir.'

'It is not possible to concentrate,'·there was a faint question in Mr Heron's voice as he stooped forward, 'when the mind is distracted by some unshared worry.'

'No, really, sir,' Dan said woodenly. 'It's nothing. I shall do the task you have set me.' He reached for the book and tried to ignore the disappointed droop of the tutor's shoulders as the old man walked out of the room.

Historia Barbae Nigrae. He wrote the words neatly and then stared down at the book, with its black print and the brown lines which defaced it. *Curious brown ink,* Mr Heron had said. Would he have disapproved even more if he knew that it was not ink? That Sal, in a dramatic moment, had underlined the words with her own blood?

In spite of himself, Dan gave a last glance over his shoulder. But the figures had disappeared and the lake was a ruffled expanse of grey under the dull November sky. Only the branches of the trees, stark and sinister with their few remaining leaves, stirred gently on the shore in the breeze that had sprung up. Shuddering slightly, Dan picked up his pen again and dipped it in the inkwell.

Feeling guilty about Mr Heron's disappointment, he worked longer than necessary on his translation, polishing it until the phrases flowed not merely correctly, but with the sort of economical elegance which pleased the old tutor. It was twelve o'clock by the time he finished and he was stiff and tired. Laying his paper on the table for Mr Heron to look over, he put away the pen and slid the battered book into its place on the shelf, running a finger slowly and affectionately down its spine.

The day had brightened and, glancing out of the window, he caught sight of a little cluster of people on the terrace behind the house. Sir Horatio was sauntering languidly with Francis on one side and Selina on the other. All his curiosity returning, Dan hurried down the stairs and went out to join them.

'A most *romantic* fancy,' Francis was drawling. 'I vow, sir, I had not thought you so whimsical.'

Sir Horatio took a pinch of snuff from his little enamelled box and smiled with self-satisfaction. 'But you must know, Francis,' he said, 'that they are all the rage. Why, the Earl himself has had one built. But not, I fancy, as excellent as mine. I studied all the best drawings and consulted many opinions. I imagine that it will be greatly admired.'

25

Selina caught Dan's eye. 'They are speaking of the hermitage in the wood,' she explained.

'*Such* a notion,' Francis smiled. 'I have a longing to see it. Shall we walk in that direction?'

He was still addressing his father and Dan, watching the group, knew that something had happened between Francis and Selina. At breakfast, Francis had been fishing for her, lingering over his words and watching her face. Now it was different. They were almost ignoring each other, but not as if they had quarrelled. Dan could feel their awareness of each other, stretched like a tight thread. Uneasily, he joined the group and they paced two and two through the gardens and down past the lake.

Francis walked ahead with Sir Horatio, and Dan heard him drawl, 'But I have not told you, sir, of what I saw last week. Perry Pemberton got us a window to view a hanging at Tyburn. It was vastly entertaining.'

'A strange entertainment to choose,' Dan muttered to Selina, 'if there is any truth in the tale of the highwayman. A hanging is a little near the bone.'

'Everything is amusing to Francis,' Selina answered absently. She was watching her elder brother's back.

'You're pleased that he has come, aren't you?' Dan said quietly.

'I would be glad of *anything* that brought some excitement into this boring life.' Selina twitched at the strings of her chip bonnet. 'Besides, Francis is like a breath of the outside world. The *real* world.' Without looking at Dan, she smiled suddenly and, bending down, picked up a stone which she shied deftly across the water of the lake. It skipped four times along the surface before sinking. Sir Horatio looked quickly back over his shoulder, but Selina's hands were folded demurely, as if they had never held anything but a fan.

They began to walk under the first trees of the wood, which threw chilly shadows across the winding path, and as they drew nearer to the hermitage, Selina's hands clasped each other more tightly. Dan watched her, saying nothing.

'My dear father,' Francis's voice came from ahead, a trifle

too enthusiastic, 'it is a most remarkable edifice.'

On the far side of a clearing, the new hermitage crouched grotesquely, low and gnarled. It was made of stone cunningly hewn to imitate giant tree roots. The windows were barred and unglazed and the roof was topped, incongruously, by a little turret where a bell hung. Beneath one of the windows, a rustic bench stood against the wall and over the door words were carved.

Ye who have wearied of the dull world's empty care
Rest here, abide awhile and breathe a fervent prayer.

Francis walked round it in an attitude of admiration. 'It gives a most powerful atmosphere to the wood.'

Sir Horatio smiled modestly. 'The inside is even more carefully designed. Shall we step in?'

They opened the heavy, studded door and entered the low room. Daniel could see them peering round at the vaulted roof and rough walls, carved craggily, like a cave.

'Shall we go in too?' he said to Selina.

'I think – no.' Her voice was oddly breathless. 'Let us sit on the bench a while and enjoy the air.'

She sat down, feet neatly together and one toe tapping the ground softly. Dan, sitting beside her, realized that they were well placed to hear what was happening inside the hermitage. Their heads were just below the level of the window.

'A most medieval feeling,' Francis was saying. 'The crucifix, the stone bench, the open hearth – most perfect of its kind.'

'Certainly,' Sir Horatio said smugly, 'I do not think I have missed anything which could add to the impression.'

'Oh yes, sir,' said Francis, as if he were surprised, 'there is one thing lacking, of course.'

Selina's foot stopped tapping suddenly.

'What is that?' Sir Horatio's voice, from inside, sounded insulted.

'Why Father, a hermit, of course.' Francis ignored Sir Horatio's disbelieving snort. 'Have you not heard of its being done? It is not common enough to be ordinary, I grant you, but imagine the effect. The gloomy wood, the austere monkish cell, and there, in the shadows, a stooping figure in a grey homespun robe.'

'Hmm.' Sir Horatio sounded thoughtful. 'Whimsical, I grant you, but not easy to achieve. One would have to find the right kind of man.'

Dan heard Selina catch her breath and hold it, and he pretended to stare away into the wood, so that she should not realize he was observing her.

'I could almost promise,' came Francis's voice, elaborately careless, 'to find you someone if you wish. I should be amused to interview prospective hermits.'

'Well –' Sir Horatio paused.

Selina did not move, and Dan stared harder at the clustered trees.

'– well, I will authorize you to do it. The county looks to me, after all, as one of the leaders of fashion and taste, and –' Sir Horatio was already preening himself, as if the whole thing had been his idea, but Dan had no chance to listen to his words. Selina had let out her breath and was babbling about the delightful view from the bench.

'Why, I can even glimpse the Hall, between the trees. I think I shall bring my paints up here and make a watercolour of the prospect.'

'You hate painting,' Dan said gruffly. 'You've always said so.'

'Ah, but you forget. That was before I became a fine young lady.'

With a brittle laugh, Selina stood up and went to meet the two men coming out of the hermitage. Studiously ignoring Francis, she listened attentively to her father, who was eager to explain the notion of the hermit. Dan frowned.

'That frown again!' Francis said softly, at his elbow. 'You don't like the plan?'

'It isn't that.' Confused, Dan said the first thing that came into his head. 'I hate to see Sal playing the young lady.'

'All the best pirates grow up into young ladies,' Francis said teasingly.

28

'But she's only pretending. She hasn't changed really.'

'Yes she has.' Francis's voice had an odd edge of sharpness to it. 'You are mistaken. She is as proper and well-behaved as Mother herself now.'

It was almost like a warning and as they walked back through the wood Dan lingered behind, watching the others thoughtfully. What was this game that Francis and Sal were playing? The question nagged at him.

As they reached the terrace again, Francis spoke to Selina at last. 'We have two hours before dinner, Sal. Shall we go for a ride?'

'I'll come too,' Dan said quickly.

Francis looked at him. 'I think not.'

'But –'

'Oh Dan, don't be a *bore*,' Selina said with nervous impatience. 'You can't come tagging along everywhere we go.'

For a moment, Dan was speechless. Until eight or nine months ago, she had dragged him after her everywhere. He remembered her last year, climbing a tree on the other side of the park, with dirt on her nose and a rip like a barn door in her petticoat. She had been yelling, 'Keep up, Morgan, me old shipmate! I can't board this vessel alone! Let's beat the lubbers to a jelly!' And now – tagging along. With quiet fury, he stalked away and up the stairs.

A quarter of an hour later, he heard Selina come out of her bedroom in her riding habit and run lightly downstairs. 'Are you ready, Francis? Let's go down to the village.'

If they went to the village, he could watch them from the nursery window. See how they behaved when they thought they were alone together. Faintly ashamed of himself, he sneaked out of his room and crept towards the stairs.

A sound behind him made him jump. Then, as he realized what it was, he smiled. The baby. Nurse must have brought it down to be fed. With any luck, he'd have the nursery to himself, with no one to ask what he was about.

Quickly, he hobbled up the stairs and into the warm clutter of the nursery. He would be able to see through the far window. There was a bundle of rags on the window-seat but, not bothering to move it, he flung himself on top of it.

Instantly, the bundle of rags yelped and punched him in the ribs.

Chapter 3

*B*ETTY had been asleep. At long last, after a night of walking up and down with the baby and a morning of washing and mending its clothes, she had found time to sit down. As she slumped on the window-seat, she felt the waves of sleep eddy round her and she huddled up and let them close over her head.

At once she had drifted back. Back to the dark, stuffy little cottage with its empty fireplace and its tightly closed windows. A fire would have meant smoke that might stain the lace. An open window would have let the dust blow in. So the girls in the lace school breathed the stale air and warmed themselves with diddy pots of hot coals tucked under their skirts. In her dream, Betty could see the light flicker, multiplied dozens of times through the water-filled glass lamps set around the candles. Long shadows moved on the walls as the girls bent over their lace pillows and Betty's sleeping fingers twitched in time to the rhythmic thrumming of the voices.

> 'Needle pin, needle pin, stitch upon stitch,
> Work the old lady out of the ditch.
> If she is not out as soon as I
> A rap on the knuckles shall come by and by.
> A horse to carry my lady about
> Must not look off till twenty are out.'

The pins moved, the lace grew, slowly, slowly, and the voices began to drag, dreary with exhaustion.

> *'Twenty miles have I to go*
> *Nineteen miles have I to go*
> *Eighteen miles have I to go. . . .'*

When Dan's body thudded on top of her, it tangled briefly with her dream. She thought they had all set on her while she dozed and she began to punch and kick, yelling, 'Mind my diddy pot! If you knock 'en, my petticoats'll burn!'

But even as she yelled, she came swimming back up through the depths of sleep and heard a voice shouting at her.

'Stop hitting me! Stop it at once!'

It was the wrong kind of voice. Her dream broke, and she realized that the fine cloth sleeve she was clutching had no place in a lace school. She dragged her eyes open and there, close to hers, was a pale face. The cripple boy's. Automatically enraged at being jerked out of her sleep, she bellowed, 'You should knock too! Snooping about! Spying at people!'

It was no way to talk. Aunt Annie would have been shocked. But before Betty could feel afraid, she saw Dan's face. It had gone even paler, startled.

'Snooping?' he said stiffly. 'Whatever do you mean?'

She knew that sort of voice. It was like their Samuel's when Mother had caught him with his fingers in the jam pot. 'Jam? What jam?' She followed Dan's quick glance out of the window and said, with sudden inspiration, 'Come to snoop at *them*, didn't 'ee?'

She jerked an accusing finger towards the gravel forecourt below, where Francis and Selina were mounting two horses.

'You are quite mistaken.' Dan looked away from the window quickly, but his cheeks went faintly pink. He was just like Samuel. Amazed to discover it, Betty forgot all caution.

'They be going riding? Wouldn't take 'ee? Don't do no good to be jealous.' Then she clapped her hand to her mouth. What was she saying? There would surely be trouble now.

But Dan was stuttering and frowning. Then suddenly, as if he had been uncorked, he began to talk awkwardly, the words stumbling over each other.

'I – you don't understand – it's not the riding. There's

32

something going on. She looks at him like – like a rabbit with a fox – and their heads together and – oh, it doesn't matter.'

He stopped abruptly, his face astonished, as if she had tricked him into talking. Betty spoke quickly, to hide his embarrassment.

'Our Mary and our Thomas, they did have that sort of carry-on once. Whispering in the chimney corner and huddling in the garden. Fair made my bones ache with trouble. Didn't do no good to talk to 'em.'

'What did you do?' Dan was watching her.

She grinned. 'Followed 'em, that's what. Caught 'em red-handed mouching Farmer Day's apples. *They* were like rabbits then. Should've seen 'em run.' She glanced out of the window, at the two horses pacing down the drive, their riders calm and upright. 'But those two are never mouching apples.'

'I wish they were!' Dan said violently. 'It's worse than that. I can *feel* it.' He sighed. 'Unless I'm going mad.'

Betty sneaked a look at his brooding face staring through the window, and wondered. Was he touched? Like poor Dick Miller, who saw his mother drown in the pond one spring and could never talk of anything else ever afterwards. ''Tes a-rising! The water's a-rising, I tell 'ee! 'Twill have us all!' She could hear him now. And that same intense, brooding gaze on his face.

'Look,' said Dan suddenly. 'They're leaving the drive. So the trees hide them from the house.'

'Can see 'em from up here.' Betty shrugged. Nothing to fuss about. The two horses were striding down the sloping park towards the hedge at the bottom. On the other side of the hedge, the road curved, white and dusty, completely empty except for a squat gig, heavy and clumsy as a pedlar's, which was rattling along from Tiverton way. 'They be riding gently,' she said in a soothing voice, to calm Dan.

'Wait.' He put a hand on her arm and, as if that were a signal, the two riders broke into a trot, glancing back over their shoulders to check that they could not be seen. The next moment, Francis urged his horse into a gallop followed helter-skelter by Selina, who raced after him between the scattered trees. Betty could see Selina's jaunty little hat sliding slowly sideways as strands of brown hair escaped and blew out behind her. For an instant Betty was almost breathless watching them, as if she herself could feel the cold wind which seared colour into Selina's cheeks. And she remembered the impatient arm flourishing round the elegant drawing-room.

'Bless her heart!' she said hotly. 'Has to keep niminy-piminy enough up here at the house. Where's the harm if her races a bit?'

'Father wouldn't be pleased if he could see her,' Dan said grimly.

Betty poked him in the ribs. 'Just out to spoil their sport, aren't 'ee? What's amiss? Can't 'ee ride with that leg?'

'Of course I can. I –'

But Betty was not listening to him any more. She leaned forward earnestly, gripping the window-ledge. 'Look! Her's not stopping. Must stop afore the hedge.'

Francis had slowed, to let Selina catch him up at the bottom of the park, but when she drew level she touched her hat in a mocking gesture and swept past, towards the gate which led through the hedge. Betty clutched at Dan's hand. 'Won't her stop?'

'Selina?' He shook his head. 'Of course she won't. She's going to jump the gate and ride straight across the common.'

'But the gig!' All the while they had been watching, Betty had been half aware of the black gig rumbling along the road towards the park gates. Now it was just behind the hedge. And Dan suddenly saw it too.

'She can't see it,' he said in a tight voice. 'Not from where she is. Sal!'

It was ridiculous to shout. Selina could never have heard. Still in the same wild, headlong flight, she put her horse at the gate and, as it rose, she glanced backwards at Francis, laughing. At the same moment, the gig on the road drew level with the gate.

It happened in a flash. Selina's horse, in mid-jump, shied sideways. The driver of the gig jerked his own horse over towards the far ditch, on the edge of the common. He avoided

34

Selina, but the gig slid into the ditch and Selina was thrown the other way, on to the road.

'Oh, Sal,' murmured Dan. Looking quickly at him, Betty saw that his face had gone quite white.

Proper fond of her, he is, she thought. She patted his hand.

'Cheer up. 'Tes none so bad. Look now, there. Her's back afoot already.'

Sure enough, Selina was brushing herself down and bending anxiously to feel her horse's legs.

'She's always the same,' Dan said shakily. 'Rushes on. Never thinks where it's leading. It's wonderful if you're with her. You can do it too. Run and run and forget that your leg hurts. We used to play at pirates together and, with her, I could scramble and climb and everything. But if you're watching –' He shuddered.

Down on the road, Francis and Selina were helping the driver push his gig out of the ditch while the horse in front strained at its harness. Before long it was on the road again, rattling on its way. Francis and Selina mounted and rode, more soberly, in the other direction

'There. See,' Betty said. 'No harm done.' Then she frowned. 'But what's he about? That one in the gig?' The black gig was turning in through the main gates and moving up the twisting drive towards the Hall. 'Cheeky devil. Pedlar or a factor, by the look of that gig. He's never coming up to complain?'

'Eh?' Still vague from shock, Dan peered out of the window. 'No, of course he's not coming to complain. This is where he was coming anyway.'

'You know who 'tes?'

''Course I do. Though I don't know what he's doing here. It's Mr Ellerby, my brother George's secretary.'

'Mr George?' Betty remembered. 'Him that's abroad, looking at ruins?'

'Yes, he's touring Europe.' Dan did not sound very interested. 'But he's not due back until next year. I expect Mr Ellerby has brought letters from him.'

'And you're not excited?' Betty looked curiously at him. 'To hear news out of foreign parts?'

'From *George*?' Unexpectedly, Dan smiled. 'He's not one for raptures. I dare say he will detail the prices of all the pictures he has seen. And Father will hold him up to us as the model of a polite, well-behaved young man. George is more boring than mutton pudding.'

Betty listened, idly watching the gig. It came round the last curve and drew up on the gravel in front of the Hall. Down climbed a short, thin man, his movements precise and economical. As he stood there waiting for the groom to come and take his horse, Betty thought that she had never seen anyone so dry and self-contained. His mouth was folded tidily, as if no unconsidered word were ever permitted to slip out of it. His dark coat was buttoned tightly to his chin, and his very wig was restricted, the tail of hair at the back tied into a neat black bag. Betty pulled a face.

'Fair makes you shudder, that one.'

'Ellerby?' Reluctantly, Dan turned his eyes away from the dwindling figures of Francis and Selina and looked down at the forecourt. 'I've never thought about him much. He's very quiet.'

'Quiet?' Betty shook her head, an odd chill creeping up her spine. 'More than quiet. A snooper. Mark my words.'

'Oh, rubbish.' Dan was calmer now, and he laughed scornfully. 'You have snooping like a maggot in your brain.'

'Me?' Betty bristled. ''Tain't me as goes peeking at folks out of windows. Sneaking about and watching a poor girl that's bored to screaming.'

'I wasn't sneaking.' Dan sounded offended. 'I was worried about her. Like you were about your brother and sister.'

Betty tossed her head. She had taken to Selina, and she thought Dan a pale-faced milk-and-water thing. 'Worried? If you were really worried, you'd find out what's afoot and put a stop to it. *If* anything's afoot.'

Dan stood up and moved away from her, his face all at once closed and secretive. 'I am sorry that I disturbed you,' he said with cold politeness. 'Do go back to sleep.'

He limped out of the room and Betty heard his feet go slowly down the stairs, the left boot sounding more than the right. He had shut her off as sharply as if he had slammed a door and for a moment she was hurt and enraged. Easy for him to dream up troubles and play hoity-toity. Never had to work all night for his living. *And* he was touched in the head, like as not. She brooded blackly, frowning out over the trees.

'Rouse thesself, wench.' It was the nurse, carrying the baby on her hip. 'Fair little fiend he's bin. Would cry. Wouldn't suck. Bless us! Take 'en off me. I need a bit of something.'

She thrust the baby at Betty as if it were a bundle of old clothes and went into the bedroom. A second later came the clink of bottle against glass, and Betty frowned and sighed. She had already forgotten about Dan and his imagined worries.

Chapter 4

*B*UT it was not so easy for Dan to forget about Betty. That peculiar girl, with her rat's-tail hair and her skinny face. She had talked to him as if he were some brother of hers. He had only been worrying about Sal, quietly, because that was his way. Hadn't he? Betty's words had made him see himself differently, as jealous and snooping, and he squirmed inwardly.

He did not think about the other things she had said until after dinner, when everyone was sitting in the drawing-room drinking tea. But then he was reminded, by the sight of Mr Ellerby, perched on one of the upright chairs and sitting as stiff and uncommunicative as a poker. Suddenly interested, Dan watched him.

'Now, Ellerby,' Sir Horatio was saying, languidly, 'I know you have brought letters from my son George. Perhaps you would care to read them aloud to us. That is if they contain nothing – unsuitable.'

'I shall be happy to read them.' Mr Ellerby inclined his neat head gravely and unfolded the papers in his hand, with a crisp movement of his fingers. The rest of his body was completely still.

Around him, everyone else was moving in some way. Lady Merrowby was pouring a cup of tea; Sir Horatio was taking a pinch of snuff; Mr Heron was nodding vaguely, his eyes attentive, but his mind full of Latin poetry. From the corner where Selina and Francis sat, Dan could feel a deeper restlessness. The two of them took no notice of each other, but Francis's fingers drummed lightly on a little table at his side and Selina was nervously twisting a ribbon. They were as impatient as two mettlesome horses, held still only by a great effort.

Mr Ellerby regarded them all with grave grey eyes, dull as pebbles, and Dan, remembering what Betty had said, wondered for the first time what lay behind those eyes. But there was no clue. Mr Ellerby coughed discreetly and began to read, in a businesslike voice.

'My dear Father and Mother, we are come at last to Genoa, after a journey remarkable for nothing save the inconvenience of the inns, at which we were obliged to put up on the way, and the rapacity of their landlords.'

'Dear boy,' murmured Lady Merrowby unguardedly. 'I hope the beds were well aired and –' She subsided into silence at a crushing look from Sir Horatio.

Mr Ellerby paused courteously until she had finished and then went on. 'Genoa is situate in a bay of excessive fineness, and set on a rising hill, with a fair prospect of the sea. The beauty of the gardens and the excellence of the architecture contribute to my pleasure in my surroundings.'

'Can it be,' drawled Francis, shifting in his chair, 'that our respected brother is developing a taste for the arts?'

'The palaces,' Mr Ellerby continued blandly, 'are of the style of Palladio and no words of mine can describe them fittingly, nor pay sufficient tribute to the many pictures which it has been my good fortune to view.'

'Isn't he going to tell us *anything*?' Selina interrupted impatiently. 'He says what everyone knows already. If I had been only two days in Italy, I could write you a book about the splendid buildings and the exquisite pictures. But George – why, he might never have been in Genoa at all!'

There was an odd, prickly silence. Then Sir Horatio held up one white finger. 'Selina. Such vehemence is unbecoming. I only wish you could behave as soberly as George.'

'Yes, Father.' Selina lowered her eyes meekly, but her fingers gave a savage twitch to her ribbon, and she glanced sideways at Francis who was tapping a toe on the ground.

Dan sympathized with them. The letters were excessively

boring. Dull letters from dull George, worthily telling them those things they already knew about Genoa, with no special observations or humorous anecdotes. Surely even George must have noticed more than that? But Mr Ellerby's voice went on evenly, matching the uninspired writing.

'I must warn you, dear Father,' he read as he approached the end of the last letter, 'that we live very retired here, not keeping company with such English people as frequent the town. Indeed, I should not be greatly astonished if they were unaware of our presence here.'

'What's that?' Sir Horatio sat up sharply, roused from his usual lethargy. 'What's the boy thinking of? Does he imagine I have sent him abroad merely to view old ruins? I meant him to seek out good company, to meet members of the nobility, people who might be of use to him when he returns home. He's got a good head and an eye to his own advantage. What's he about, Ellerby?'

'Sir Horatio,' Mr Ellerby murmured, 'I beg you to remember the sobriety of your eldest son's conduct. He is only too well aware of the dangers of associating with those to whom money is of no account. Reputation is more lightly held abroad, and fortunes have been lost, I assure you, by young men who did not watch their company and spent too much time at the card tables.'

'Hrmph!' Sir Horatio took another pinch of snuff and flicked his fingers fastidiously. 'I suppose I should be grateful to have one son who lives within his income.' He relieved his irritation by glaring across at Francis.

'Indeed, sir,' Francis sounded gently amused, 'I swear I have been greatly improved by my brother's letters. I wait eagerly for the rest.'

Mr Ellerby coughed. 'In fact, that is all, Sir Horatio. Except, of course, for sentiments of family affection.'

Sir Horatio frowned, annoyed at being cheated out of the foreign gossip he had expected. To vent his feelings, he waved a hand at Dan. 'Well, you may as well go to bed then, Daniel.'

'I too.' Francis rose suddenly to his feet. 'If you will forgive me. I am feeling the effects of my journey yesterday.'

As if he had signalled to her, Selina got up with a yawn and followed him to the door.

'I also have come a long way,' Mr Ellerby said quickly. 'Perhaps you will forgive me, Sir Horatio.'

Sir Horatio looked at them all in amazement. 'But it is only half-past nine.' He was accustomed to sit for hours over his tea. 'Well, we shall look over the letters again.' And he fixed Lady Merrowby and Mr Heron with a glare, forbidding them to desert him.

Francis and Selina slid quickly out of the door. Dan was held up as Mr Ellerby bowed and handed over the papers and it was almost a minute before he and the secretary emerged into the entrance hall. It was empty, with no sound of footsteps on the stairs.

But the morning-room door stood slightly ajar and Dan suddenly had an odd fancy that there were people behind that door. As if Francis and Selina were waiting there, to escape being watched.

Even more oddly, Mr Ellerby, too, looked towards the morning-room door, pausing while his dull eyes scanned it and his tongue-tip flicked across his lips. 'Miss Selina has become a most proper, refined young lady,' he murmured, almost to himself, frowning thoughtfully at the door.

'But she's still wild at heart.' Dan smiled grimly. 'You know that.'

He was thinking of her mad ride across the gate and into the gig. But Mr Ellerby did not respond. His eyes glanced at Dan and grew colder. 'I'm sure,' he said icily, 'that her behaviour is always admirable.'

Dan opened his mouth. Then shut it again, puzzled.

'You will wish to go straight to bed, of course,' said Mr Ellerby, still chilly. It was almost an order.

'Of course,' Dan said automatically. 'Good-night, Mr Ellerby.' But he was disturbed by something strange in the secretary's manner. Limping up the stairs, he paused on the curve of the first landing, when he was in shadow, and peered back over the banisters.

There was a soft sound as the morning-room door opened

wider. Mr Ellerby stepped quietly back into a shadowy corner, hidden by a statue. Not noticing him, Francis and Selina slid out of the morning-room, glanced towards the closed drawing-room door and quickly crossed the marble floor of the hall. A second later, they had slipped through the front door and out into the night.

Walking? At this hour? Dan frowned in the darkness. Then he saw something even stranger. Mr Ellerby crossed the hall, padding on silent feet. Pulling aside the heavy curtain, he looked through a window, nodding gently. Then he, too, let himself noiselessly out of the front door.

Curious, Dan crept down the stairs and, in his turn, pulled the curtain aside. In the dark he could see shadows moving down the drive. Two close together, hurrying over the gravel. And a third black shape lagging behind and walking cautiously on the grass at the side, beneath the trees.

For a moment Dan was absorbed by the oddity of it all. Then, suddenly, he seemed to see himself, crouching and peering, and he heard Betty's scornful voice again. '*Worried? If you were really worried, you'd find out what's afoot.*' Almost without deciding, he opened the front door. Tiptoeing across the gravel in front of the Hall, he too stepped on to the grass beside the drive. Francis and Selina were almost swallowed up in the darkness ahead, but he could see Mr Ellerby's figure, moving briskly, and he set himself to follow that.

It was hard to keep pace. They were walking so fast that he had to break into a limping run from time to time. But it was easy to see where they were going. First Francis, then Selina, then Mr Ellerby, took the sunken lane which ran between high banks towards the village. The roots of the trees bulged in twisted shapes from the banks, making deep shadows as if black figures crouched all the way along. Shuddering slightly, Dan kept close to them as he followed.

Suddenly, Mr Ellerby looked back over his shoulder. Dan froze, his face against the earth bank. His shape must have been visible in the moonlight, but it merged with the roots, as if he were another tree, and, after a breath, Mr Ellerby turned away and continued his pursuit. Dan crept behind even more

42

carefully, his feet making no sound on the dusty road.

As they came into the village, he loitered behind a tree, letting the other three draw ahead of him until he could tell where they were going. There was a little more light now, odd rays from an uncurtained window here and there. In the gleam, Dan could see Francis and Selina hurrying in the shadows. Half-way through the village, they reached the crazy, huddled buildings of the British Lion, the only inn in the village. Its front windows were bright and from the parlour came a sound of loud voices and the occasional quarrelsome shout.

Francis, taking Selina's hand to pull her after him, moved down the alley at the side of the inn. Through the darkness, Dan heard a gentle double tap. There was a burst of light in the blank side wall as a door opened, outlining the two tall, slender figures. Then they stepped inside and there was darkness again.

Mr Ellerby moved quietly down the street. This time there was no tap, no sudden light. He seemed to melt into the shadows round the British Lion and disappear.

Dan crouched on, beside his tree, puzzling. If he went on, he might be caught, trapped in the alley. But if he went back, he might never find out what was going on. And he was sure now that there was something going on. Why else should Francis bring Selina, in the darkness and in secret, to a place she would never be permitted to visit openly?

Dan inched cautiously along the street, jerking to a stop every time a door opened or a voice sounded. As he drew near the inn, there was a huge burst of laughter and the front door was flung wide. Quickly he stepped into the dark alley at the side and leaned close against the building, the rough wall grazing his cheek. A couple of men sauntered out of the parlour and walked through the village talking.

When they had disappeared, Dan looked up and down the alley. There was no sign of Mr Ellerby and the door in the side wall was tightly shut. He sidled along, alert for any movement in the shadows, and put his ear to the edge of the door, trying to catch some noise from inside.

It was a solid oak door and the voices on the other side were

43

muffled and indistinct. He could not make out any words, but he could catch the rise and fall of sound as people spoke and he strained his ears, trying to hear some higher tone that might, perhaps, be Selina's voice.

There! Or was it? He pressed closer to the door and it gave a sudden creak as it took his weight. He was horrified, but he did not dare move away, in case it creaked again. Chilly and afraid, he waited for the sound of quick feet hurrying to fling it open and reveal him crouched there. But there was no check in the voices. They must have been making too much noise inside to have heard.

It was almost five minutes before he realized his mistake. He was just deciding that he would do no good there, that he might just as well go home to bed, when it happened. There was no warning, no sound of footsteps or of the latch lifting.

Completely unexpectedly, the door flew open. Unable to stop himself, Dan staggered through it and across the floor. There was a bellow of raucous laughter from all round the room, thudding under the low ceiling. Looking about him, Dan saw ten or a dozen men, grinning and scarred, all mocking him. All strangers.

Slowly he straightened. He was in a little room at the back of the inn. Three or four doors opened off it, and it was roughly furnished with a table and odd chairs. On every chair lounged one of the fierce looking strangers, with a mug of beer at his elbow. It seemed impossible that Selina could have been here. These men were not like the deferential villagers she sometimes visited. They were dirty and villainous, with bold eyes. And as the laughter died away, those eyes settled on Dan with a growing hardness.

He stammered the first thing that came into his head. 'I'm sorry. I – I was looking for my sister.'

'Looking for his sister!' The man who had opened the door, a great hulk with broken teeth, laughed sarcastically. ''Tes just the place.'

'Here I be, brother dear!' Another man, wiry and wrinkled, stood up from the table and minced a few steps, holding up an imaginary petticoat and twisting his face to a simper.

'No, here!'

'No, *here*!'

Men lurched towards him, prinking, thrusting huge, beer-smelling faces at him. They loomed nightmarishly and Dan staggered backwards until he was pressed against the door, gazing round in bewilderment.

Suddenly, a mug thudded heavily on the table. Instantly, the men stopped their game and looked sheepishly round. Dan had not even noticed the gaunt old man sitting at the far end of the table, hunched in the shadows. But as he spoke now, the whole room was still.

'Sit down.' His voice was a harsh croak, not above a whisper, but instantly the men slunk back to their seats and watched him, waiting.

He was thin and grey, his cheeks hollow under prominent cheek-bones the colour of cheese. On either side of his face, lank strands of hair straggled over his shoulders, and his eyes, sunken but bright, looked Dan up and down.

'Come here, boy.' His voice was still a whisper, but it was more chilling than a shout.

Slowly, clenching his hands behind his back, to hide their trembling, Dan limped across the floor to stand facing the old man. The grey eyes scanned him again. The thin lips smiled slightly.

'Fine hobbledehoy us've caught.'

Dan lifted his head. 'My name is Daniel Merrowby.' Let them know they should not dare attack him. 'Son of Sir Horatio Merrowby of Linhay Hall.'

One or two of the men glanced quickly at each other, but the old man's stare did not waver. 'Brave work to find 'ee at, then. Listening at doors!'

'I was looking for my sister,' Dan said stoutly. 'I saw her come in here.'

This time there was no laughter. Only the sharpness of the grey eyes resting on his face. 'Saw her, did 'ee? And her a young lady. Ay, 'tes likely as her'd walk in here among all these.' The whisper rasped scornfully.

'I –' Dan faltered and stopped. He was certain she had come

in here. He had seen her. And she could have been here and slipped away. There were plenty of other doors out of the room. But the cold eyes drew words from him without his willing it. 'I must have been mistaken.'

The old man nodded, and his thin, wet lips pressed tight. 'Mistaken, surely. You listened at the door for nothing, then?'

'I didn't listen. That is –'

Slowly the narrow lips curved into a sour smile. 'Oh, you listened right enough. Heard nothing, though, did 'ee? I know it. I be no fool, to talk behind thin doors. You heard nothing.' He paused, his face cunning. 'And what did 'ee see, then?'

His words hissed in the silence and for a moment Dan did not understand what he meant. He looked back, bewildered, with his mouth half open.

'Leave 'en, Zak.' The huge man who had opened the door shifted uncomfortably on his chair. 'Poor soul. Can't 'ee see as he's simple?'

Dan was used to that mistake. Used to denying it with quiet dignity. But now he was held speechless by Zak's eyes and it was the old man who spoke, still staring at Dan.

'Simple or wise,' he whispered, 'he'll see what I tells 'en. And not see when he's told. Like the rest of 'ee. Well, boy?'

This time Dan knew what was expected. And the room and the harsh faces were so like a nightmare that it seemed almost true. 'I have seen nothing,' he said dully. 'No one.'

Zak nodded slowly, satisfied. 'Bin walking round the village in the dark, then? For nothing?'

'That's right,' Dan said, with desperate quickness. 'It was just a fancy, a whim.' What did it matter what he said if only he could escape, be alone to think?

But he was not to be let go yet. Without looking down, Zak moved slightly and, following the movement, Dan saw a long, curved knife between his hands. As he turned it over thoughtfully, the blade caught the light, glancing brightness on to Dan's horrified face.

''Tes a strange thing –' the ugly whispering voice sounded almost amused – 'but folks have a way of keeping promises as are made to me. I never joke. I never threaten. But what I say, 'tes done.' Over and over went the knife blade between the old, gnarled hands. 'Can 'ee understand it?'

Dan looked slowly round at the men who had obeyed so meekly and nodded, his throat dry with terror.

'Off with 'ee, then. And remember. See nothing, hear nothing – and sleep sound.'

As quickly as he could, Dan stumbled towards the door and out into the darkness. Panting, he limped up the village street towards the hollow lane. Although he had not been touched, his whole body ached as if huge fists had pummelled him, and he hobbled the whole way at a half-run as if feet followed him.

When he had stumbled up the steps to the front door of the Hall, he found that it was locked. Of course. Anxious only to get inside, in the light, he beat on it with his fists, not caring what anyone might think. Thomas, the footman, raised his eyebrows as he opened it, but Dan did not pause to explain. He clattered up the wide stairs and along the landing.

As he passed Francis's door, it opened suddenly. Francis stood there in his bedgown, as elegant and languid as if he had not been out at all. Looking Dan up and down, from his panting face to his muddy shoes, he shuddered mockingly.

'Walking in the dark, Daniel? What strange notions you have.' The voice was light, but the green eyes were thoughtful.

Dan did not stop to answer. He crashed into his own bedroom, tore off his clothes and scrambled into bed, curling his icy toes into the cosy space where the warming-pan had been. But it was a long while before he slept. He lay awake, rigid and sweating, and the same words pounded over and over in his head. 'I was right. There *is* something going on. I was right. I was right.'

But there was no triumph in the knowledge. It was a weight as dense and heavy as the thick shadows which crowded the corners of the room, oppressing his sleepless eyes.

It was a few days later that the man in the brown coat received his letter. This time he was sitting alone in the back room of the French inn. He broke the seal and unfolded the crackling paper, smoothing it on the table. As he read, he frowned slightly. Then suddenly, although he was alone, he laughed aloud.

'So,' he murmured, 'it is arranged.'

He poured himself a glass of wine from the bottle at his elbow and sat sipping it slowly while he picked up the letter he had just read. Holding it over the candle, he watched the flame lick at it. There was a wisp of smoke and then a swift flare which lit up his plump, expressionless face. Dropping the paper on to the floor, he ground out the flames with his heel and the smoke curled lazily round the back of his boot.

Chapter 5

BETTY's wet hands were sore with cold. As she hung up the baby's clouts to dry, a raw November wind whipped her skin to chaps. Proper foul job it was. And a proper foul day too, with Aunt Annie tired as a rag and already in a black gloom. There'd be trouble with her before much longer. Frowning, Betty tweaked at the pile of wet clothes in the basket and one flicked out and fell on the earth.

'Dang it!' She scooped it up and wiped her muddy fingers on her apron. The reddish earth stained the rough skin of her hand and suddenly, as clear as if she heard it, Mother Lambert's whine came back to her, nagging the little ones in the lace school.

'Clean hands, wenches, and no dirt on the lace. If I white 'en up with all the starch in Devon, that factor'll still spot 'en if 'tes stained.'

In spite of her bad temper, Betty grinned. Bloody factor. Well out of his way she was, even if she had to wash filthy clouts. Plague of their lives he'd always been. With Mam crouched over her lace pillow on cut-off day, muttering, 'No dinner till this flounce be ended, or there'll be no money from the factor tonight.'

Poor Mam. Hard at it all the time. And Grammer there to remind her what she'd come to at last. Betty remembered Grammer, her eyes grown dim from the lace working, bending over Samuel's cradle when he was born. The gnarled, liver-spotted hands had fluttered gently over the baby's purple face, and Grammer had been crying because she could not see him.

It all came back so plainly that for a moment Betty stopped working and crouched with her hands in the wet, cold washing. And her eyes misted up with the blindness that threatened all of those who worked at the lace.

'Hey!' A hand rattled at her elbow. 'Can't you hear me?'

She came to. 'Get away!' she said fiercely, thinking it was the kitchen boy come to tease her.

'Why are you always angry?'

She looked round, straightened and bobbed a quick curtsey. 'Beg pardon, Master Daniel. Didn't know 'twas 'ee.' A fair sight he looked, too. Dark, hollow eyes, worse than Aunt Annie's, and his pale face all of a twitch. 'Seen a ghost, have 'ee?'

'I've seen –' He stopped, opened his mouth, stopped again.

Impatiently, Betty took the rest of the clothes from the basket and began to hang them. 'Bin having more fancies?'

'They're not fancies,' he said hotly. His face was flushed now. 'I was right. There is something happening. Something very wrong. But I can't say –'

'What's the use of babbling on, then?' Betty was weary and short-tempered. 'Thought you'd come to tell.'

'I promised not to.' His eyes shifted uneasily. 'But I must talk to someone and – oh, it can't matter if I tell *you*.'

'Proper polite,' she said acidly. 'Who'd 'ee promise, then?' She spread the last few clothes and picked up the basket.

'An awful old man,' Dan gulped. 'With a whispering voice.'

Slowly, Betty put the basket down again. 'What man?' she said, not looking at him.

Dan gulped again. 'They called him Zak, and he had a knife, and –'

'Dear God!' Betty was suddenly whiter than he was. 'A whispering old man? With grey hair hanging and a hollow face?'

'You know him?' Dan gripped her shoulder. 'Who is he?'

'Don't 'ee know?' Betty shuddered. ''Tes a different world you rich folk live in. I've known about 'en all my life. Peered through the curtains at 'en, many's the time. And heard the tales. Since I was so high as a kitten.'

50

'Who is he?' Dan shook at her arm. 'You must tell me. Francis and Selina went to the British Lion to meet him last night.'

'Your sister? Went to meet Whispering Zak?' Betty's eyes widened. ''Tes trouble for certain, then.'

'Who is he?'

She leaned closer to him, whispering herself. ''Tes round Honiton way he works mostly. Where I come from. He's – well, there's a hundred tales. Robberies, night-ridings, murders even. But 'tes mostly running contraband. They do say –' her voice sank even lower – 'that he whispers like that because a Riding Officer's bullet caught 'en in the throat one time. But he escaped and lived.' She shuddered again. ''Tes wonderful how he always escapes. As if 'twas the devil hisself.'

'He never gets caught?' Dan frowned at her. 'Even though people know what he does?'

'Hah!' Betty snatched up her basket. 'Think there's any as'd lay information against Zak? Knows everything, he does, about everyone, and their friends, and their kin. And the man that turned 'en in wouldn't have long to live. He –' She hunted for words, but could find none to explain to someone like Dan. How could he ever understand the way Whispering Zak lay like a long shadow across the lives of the cottage people? 'If Miss Selina went to meet 'en apurpose, her's mad. You must tell someone. Your father?'

'Father?' Dan laughed bitterly. 'He'd just lock Sal up for ever, or marry her off quickly to some old man. Besides, I promised not to tell, and there was a knife –' He hung his head and let his voice die away. 'You must tell, Betty. Tell Selina what you know and –'

'Me?' Betty began to march across the yard, trying to escape from him. 'Think I'd tangle with Whispering Zak when there's no call?'

'But you've got to! It's the only way.' All up the back stairs to the nursery he followed, nagging at her. But Betty stumped silently ahead, her chin high and her face stubborn.

As she pushed open the nursery door, she was greeted by the baby's thin wails. Still at it, was he? She scooped him up

51

and began to pat his back automatically. Where was Aunt Annie, then?

'Betty, you must help me.' Dan was still pleading. 'She's my sister, and she has no sense. You saw, the other day, how she runs straight into danger.'

''Tes just another of those games of hern,' Betty said scornfully. 'Like pirates. If you want her told, tell her yourself.'

Her tone was definite, final. Dan's body sagged and he walked slowly across to the door.

'I'll have to try, then. But I don't suppose she'll believe me. She –' He broke off as a sudden loud crash came from the bedroom. 'Whatever –'

Starting forwards, he caught hold of the bedroom door latch and, before Betty could stop him, he had flung the door wide and was staring in.

She knew what he was seeing even before she got there. Didn't take much guessing. Aunt Annie must have been having a quick lie down. Must have dozed off. When she woke, bleary and shaking, she would have reached for the gin bottle. She always said a little drink set her on her feet. But she had staggered and gone over. Now she was lying muzzily on the floor, the broken bottle in her hand and a sweet, sickly trail of gin running across the floor.

'You leave her be!' Laying the baby on the bed, Betty began to heave the old nurse to her feet, talking fiercely over her shoulder to Dan. 'Her's an old woman as nursed 'ee well, and her's tired to the marrow. Don't dare tell on her! Her'll be sent packing, with nowhere to go.'

Only half awake still, the nurse was screwing up her eyes, trying to see who stood in the doorway. Dan was quite still, an odd expression on his face. A kind of sick, pitying excitement.

'You don't care for her?' Betty said sharply.

Dan spoke at last, his mouth twisting, his voice rough and desperate. 'You'll talk to Sal, then? Tell her what you told me? *Today.*'

Choking, he spun away, leaving Betty on her knees with her mouth open.

52

So it was that, come two o'clock, Betty stood outside Selina's bedroom door, tugging her apron straight. She had always been one to speak her mind, and Selina was in there alone. Yet how could she? How could she go in and say –? But there was Aunt Annie to think of.

As if she had not willed it, her hand rose and tapped on the wood of the door.

'Come in!' It was a lively, excited voice. Selina stood with her back to her, in her petticoats. 'You're early, Molly. I'm not quite ready to dress for dinner yet.' Then she turned and saw Betty standing in the doorway. 'Oh, it's you? What do you want?'

Carefully, Betty stepped inside and shut the door. 'Please, miss, I've got something to say. Something private.'

'Private?' Selina raised her eyebrows, amused. 'Well, you haven't seen me climb any more trees, have you?' She spun round, twirling her skirts. 'Oh, I have been such a model young lady.'

Betty's throat was dry. 'Please, miss, 'tes about – 'tes about Whispering Zak.'

Selina stopped in mid-spin and sat down hard on the bed.

Betty took a step forward and swallowed. 'Come from up Honiton way I do, miss. Us all knows Zachary up there.'

Selina's eyes were wide and her whole body was rigid, except the hands which trembled in her lap. 'Why have you come?' she said stiffly.

Betty had not thought how to explain without betraying Aunt Annie or Dan. 'I – I was sent,' she muttered.

'Oh!' Suddenly, to her amazement, Selina flung back her head and let out a huge breath of relief, clasping her hands to her chest. 'Oh, you silly girl, you had me so frightened. I thought my heart would stop. I was not expecting you so soon.'

'Miss?' Betty was puzzled, but Selina went chattering on.

'I thought Zachary meant me to find a messenger of my own. I was at my wits' end, thinking whom to trust. I never dreamed he had someone already in the house. The man's as cunning as the devil!'

'There's some as says he *is* the devil,' Betty murmured

blackly, but Selina only laughed and jumped off the bed.

'I don't doubt Francis can manage him. He seemed very respectful when we saw him.' She went across to her pillow and fished out a piece of paper. 'I'm glad you're here, because there's a letter to go to him, and it will be safer if I don't take it myself. There you are.'

'Miss?'

'You know the route, don't you?'

All the time Selina rattled on, Betty had been thinking. If she fell in with this mistake, she might find out what was afoot. But if she told the real reason for her visit, now, Selina would likely seek ways to stop her mouth. Lowering her gaze, Betty muttered, 'You were to explain it, miss.'

'A fiendishly clever plan of Francis's.' Selina gave a conspiratorial smile. 'He persuaded my father that we should have a real live hermit in the hermitage in the wood. And he said he would engage the man himself. So now, in our own grounds, there is a link between us and Zachary.' She flourished the paper triumphantly. 'And here are my measurements, all neatly written out, for you to take to the holy hermit. Can you go straight away?'

''Tain't so easy, miss.' Betty frowned. ''Tes odd for a rocker to go wandering in the park.'

'Oh, take the baby.' Selina waved a hand carelessly. 'Then you can say you're giving him some fresh air. Nurse was always a great one for fresh air. If you go quickly, before it's dark, there'll be no questions.'

Automatically, Betty reached out for the paper and stuffed it down the front of her dress.

'Go quickly!' Selina was pink with excitement. 'There's so little time to arrange everything.'

At the door, Betty paused. ''Tes like a game to 'ee, miss,' she said slowly. It seemed madness to her that anyone should meddle with Whispering Zak for fun. But Selina did not take it as a criticism. She flung up her head, and her eyes sparkled as if she were a young officer, eager for battle.

'Oh, it's the *best* game! The best game I ever played in my life!'

'Hush up, little toad!' Betty rocked the baby fiercely in her arm as she slipped into the wood. The baby did not like fresh air. Its face wrinkled in furious, noisy protest. 'Hush up!'

Although it was still light, the shadows were long in the wood and the air was frosty around her ankles. She kept telling herself that it was simple, what she had to do. Deliver the letter and leave. But all she could think of was her mother, smiling as she said goodbye to her. 'Now mind and be a good wench, Betty. 'Tes a fine chance to escape all this.' The wave of her hand had taken in the lace pillow, the hovel of a cottage, even the shadow of Whispering Zak. What would she say if she could see her daughter now?

Gulping air, Betty marched along the winding path, with the baby whimpering itself into silence. She had never come so far into the wood and when she reached the clearing she paused uncertainly. Could that be the place? It was worse made than their cottage, queer and rugged. Shaking her head at the strange ways of the rich, she padded across the open space.

There was no sign of anyone. Not daring to peer through the window bars, she knocked softly on the studded door.

'. . . nominy dominy,' came a whisper from inside. The door creaked open and a tall figure in a long grey robe stood there, its matted hair lank round its face. 'Yes, my child?' The voice was benevolent, a holy hermit's whisper.

Betty clutched at the doorpost to steady herself. She had not thought it would be him. Himself. For a moment, she could not speak.

With a benign air, the old man laid a hand on her head. 'Why do 'ee come seeking the old hermit of the woods?'

The feel of his heavy hand made her dizzy. Gripping the door-frame harder, she gasped, 'Miss Selina sent me. A letter.'

Instantly the kindly expression was replaced by cold shrewdness. 'Inside!' croaked Zak, standing back for her to enter. The hermitage was dark, and long shadows staggered across its uneven ceiling. Betty fumbled quickly in the baby's wrappings, where she had hidden the letter.

'Here 'tes.' She thrust it at him.

He unfolded it and ran his eyes over the writing. 'As neat a young lady as I ever did work with.'

'If you please –' Betty was eager to leave, but he stood between her and the door, showing no inclination to move. Instead, he pulled the wrappings back from the baby's head and looked down, smiling. But there was nothing tender in his smile.

'So young,' he murmured, 'and carrying letters for old Zak already. Merrowby brat?'

Speechless, Betty nodded and Zak gave a dry chuckle. 'Have 'em all, I will,' he said, half to himself. 'All the soft, idle brood.' Suddenly he looked sharply up at Betty. 'And thee's her messenger? Where do 'ee come from?'

'I – I'm the rocker,' stuttered Betty. 'As helps the nurse.'

'So.' Frowning, the old man leaned closer and peered at her in the dim light. 'I thought 'twould be her maid. Someone close to her. How can she be sure of 'ee?' He gnawed at his knuckle for a moment. 'Where do 'ee come from afore here?'

'Up Honiton way,' Betty said faintly.

The effect of her reply was frightening. Zak whirled round and caught her face between his hard, cold hands, the fingers rough on her cheek-bones. 'Honiton way? And mixed with this? Can I trust 'ee for sure?' His eyes glittered. The candle-light sent the shadow of his nose askew across his face and drew deep grooves between his crooked teeth.

'There's no one –' Betty gulped, terrified, 'no one from up Honiton as'd dare give 'ee away.'

He nodded with satisfaction, more at her obvious fright than at what she said. Letting go of her face, he felt all along her arm, as if she were a chicken he had a mind to eat. 'Feel it in thy flesh I can,' he rasped. 'Fear and trembling. Thee'd be foolish to stop being afeard.'

'I know it,' she said faintly.

'Good.' He kept a hand on her wrist for a moment, to feel her pulse racing. 'Show me the baby again.'

Helplessly, she held out the child. She was not fond of it. It meant broken nights and hard work to her. All the same, she shivered in case Zachary's look should somehow blight it. He stroked its cheek with long, cold fingers and it actually smiled, a fuzzy, vague smile, and cooed. Instantly, the long fingers turned to pincers and nipped the round cheek cruelly.

As the baby yelled, Zachary looked down at it with a dark, brooding face. 'Us be all born to sorrow and deception,' he said gravely. 'Rich or poor. Eh, wench?'

'Yes. Oh, yes. Please –' Betty said desperately, 'please can I go now, afore I be missed?'

He nodded and stepped aside. 'And mind. Say nothing.' For a second he looked at her, and then he shook his head slowly. 'Proper sad it be. A Honiton girl mixed with this.' And as she walked out he looked at her with unmistakable disgust.

But there was no time to worry on that. She pushed past him, out of the door, and began to run back through the wood. It was all she could do to slow her feet to a becoming pace when she emerged into the open.

She felt as though her whole body were covered with clammy, evil sweat and she wanted nothing more than to wash and scrub at her skin until it was clean. But when she reached the nursery Aunt Annie was awake and alert, ready to set her to work. She had no time to herself until the family's dinner was over and nurse and baby went downstairs.

As soon as the door closed, Betty raced to the bowl of water in the corner and began to splash it all over her face, her forearms and her chest, wetting the top of her bodice. The water was icy cold, but she splashed and splashed until her skin felt raw and shaking. Then, seizing a towel, she began to rub herself dry with vicious strokes, scrubbing and scrubbing at her cheeks where Zachary had held them in his hands.

All at once, she heard the door creak and the sound of a step. Lowering the towel, she looked up. A slight, misshapen figure stood in the doorway.

'Well?' said Dan urgently. 'Have you done it? Have you spoken to her?'

Chapter 6

FRANCIS was walking in the Orangery. Standing in the bare garden, where the potted orange trees were set in summer, Dan watched his brother pacing up and down behind the long range of tall windows. Backwards and forwards he went, his fair curls showing pale between the dark green leaves of the stiff little orange trees which were housed there for the winter. In his hand he held a small silver dish of dried apricots, and every now and then he nibbled at one with disdainful greed.

No need to be nervous, Dan told himself firmly. It was only Francis. And he ought to speak to Francis, now that his attempt to warn Selina had failed. Yesterday evening, Betty had been hysterical, her scrawny face contorted desperately.

'Yes, I've spoken to her,' she had muttered. 'Won't do no good. Us'd better keep off, I tell 'ee. 'Tes too much for us to go meddling in.' And she had clutched at his sleeve with the strength of terror. 'And don't 'ee go telling as I warned 'ee about Whispering Zak. Best not talk about me at all. Please!'

He could not even find out what had frightened her. He only knew that she was helpless with shock. If any warning was to be given, he must give it himself. And there was Francis walking in the Orangery.

Limping down the path, Dan pushed open the glass door. The comfortable warmth from the stoves enfolded him.

'Francis.'

'Daniel.' Francis smiled benignly. 'Have an apricot.'

Mechanically, Dan took it and held it in his hand. 'I must talk to you.'

Francis raised an eyebrow, and Dan lowered his head stubbornly and spoke the speech he had prepared in his mind.

'I don't know why you came here, but I know it has something to do with Sal. I think you're leading her into danger.' It sounded idiotic, but he made himself go on to the end. 'You're involving her with bad company and trouble.'

'So?' The other eyebrow went up and Francis bit into an apricot. He looked amused. 'I thought you had always led her into danger yourself. What was it? Boarding enemy ships? Sacking cities? And were Blackbeard and Henry Morgan not bad company for a young lady?'

'Don't be silly. That was only a game.'

'So now she plays my games instead of yours.' Francis shrugged. 'We ride. We talk. And now we plan an expedition to see the sunrise from Hightop Hill. Ah, you hadn't heard of that? Well, it is innocent enough, I think.'

'It's not that I'm talking about.' Dan hesitated and then gabbled on. 'You took her down to the village at night. To the British Lion. I followed you. I saw you.'

'How very clever of you.' Francis sounded unsurprised. But his green eyes were sharp. 'And what else did you see?'

Too late, Dan realized that he had talked himself into a trap. He remembered Zachary's knife on the table and Betty pleading *'And don't 'ee go telling as I warned 'ee.'* He looked down. 'I saw nothing.'

'If you see nothing,' Francis said smoothly, 'it is best to say nothing. Especially with an affliction like yours.'

'What do you mean?'

Francis's smile was edged with spite. 'When the body is crippled, it is easy for people to believe that the mind is crippled too. Surely you have noticed that? And if you suddenly begin to talk nonsense –'

It was an idle threat. But Dan's mouth went dry at the tone of his brother's voice. He had to force himself to go on speaking. 'But don't you care about Sal?'

Francis's expression flickered. 'Do you know what Sal reminds me of, now she is tight-laced into propriety?' he said softly. 'I saw it as soon as I came back. And you would have seen it too, if your leg had let you follow me to school. One of the masters there kept a kestrel in a cage. It didn't flap. It didn't tear at the bars. Just sat there, decorously still. But its eyes –' He shuddered. 'It would have been happier perhaps if it had been truly tame. And Sal would certainly be safer if she grew demure and stolid, like a good cloth merchant's grand-daughter. But *I* would have freed that kestrel if I could. Trained it, and flown it from my wrist.'

That was his excuse to himself, thought Dan. Francis smiled, his calm recovered, and picked up the last apricot.

'I think you would be most unwise,' he said carelessly, 'to talk to Sal as you have talked to me. She has grown out of her games with you. Let her alone and work at your Virgil like a good boy. Instead of behaving like a jealous baby.'

Flicked into anger, Dan opened his mouth to deny the accusation. Then he thought better of it and stamped out of the Orangery, banging the glass door dangerously behind him. As he limped up the path, he realized that he was still holding the circle of dried apricot in his hand. Disgusted, he flung it away into the bushes. But his pale face was set obstinately. Francis had been lying. Whatever was going on was something worse than an early morning trip to Hightop Hill, and he could not give up until he had tried everything to stop it. Determinedly he went to look for Selina.

She was sitting in the morning room with their mother. The two of them were working at embroidery, their heads bent industriously over the frames.

'Ah, Daniel.' Lady Merrowby looked up. 'Will you ring for Thomas?'

Dan shook the heavy brass bell on the side table and while his mother murmured to the footman, 'Tea, Thomas, and please find Mr Heron to ask him if he would like some,' he moved across and sat beside Selina.

'Sal, I need to talk to you,' he muttered.

Her needle jabbed at the pattern of flowers with restless impatience and he hoped that she might come in the garden and walk with him. But all she said was, 'I want to finish this spray this afternoon. You can talk to me here.'

Dan looked furtively at his mother. She was paying them no attention, but she could hear every word they said now that Thomas had gone. He thought quickly. 'Shall I tell you about the piece of the *Aeneid* I have been reading with Mr Heron?'

Selina looked up briefly. It was an old trick of theirs for secret conversation. One from their pirate days. But Dan had not used it for nearly a year. He could not tell what she thought, because she glanced down immediately, but her needle jerked and stabbed her finger. Dan started to talk, keeping his voice casual. There was no danger that Lady Merrowby would suspect. She did not know any more about the *Aeneid* than she did about hoeing turnips.

'It's the bit where Aeneas sits fretting in his tent,' he said. Selina gave an involuntary nod of understanding. Aeneas always meant Dan himself. 'There is a stranger in the camp.' Dan paused momentarily, to make up a suitable quotation. 'You know the bit. It goes "Then, golden-curled, the tall young warrior from the far-off city strode among the tents of the sons of Troy, plotting mischief to the daughters of that ancient place."'

Selina nodded again, but slowly. She had recognized that he was talking about Francis. On the other side of the room, Lady Merrowby nodded approvingly at the subject of their conversation. Dan thought he could safely go on.

'Then' – he made himself sound enthusiastic – 'there's a lovely piece when Aeneas warns his sister.' He sat up straighter and recited as if from a translation: '"Sister mine, dearer to me than life, do you not know the danger which surrounds you? This man, he of the golden curls and the smooth tongue, will take you to strange places in the darkness, leading you among false friends with rough faces and treachery in their hearts."'

Selina pulled at her needle and muttered impatiently as the material cockled.

'Pay attention to your work,' Lady Merrowby said mildly. 'However interesting you find Daniel's conversation, you should control your enthusiasm.'

'Oh, it's not that, mother,' said Selina, in a clear, tense voice.

'I think this Virgil is stupid stuff. I'm only too glad that I am a girl and need not take any notice of it.'

She looked challengingly at Dan. There was no mistaking the rebuff. She was not prepared to listen to him. Miserably he watched her continue her sewing with quick untidy stitches. At that moment the door opened and the old tutor walked in, followed by Thomas with the tea things.

'Ah, Mr Heron.' Lady Merrowby waved him graciously to a chair. 'We have been enjoying the results of your work. Daniel has been entertaining us by reciting the translation he is making with you at the moment. A story of Aeneas and his sister.'

'His sister?' Startled, the tutor looked across at Daniel, who felt his face grow red. But Mr Heron only murmured, 'I am glad to have a pupil who takes such pleasure in the works of the poets. I hope he will enjoy preparing the passage I have set him to construe before dinner.' There was not even any curiosity in his voice. He was a man who believed in privacy.

Selina yawned and stood up. 'I have finished my spray, mother. I think I shall take a stroll in the gardens. I believe I can see Francis walking in the Orangery.'

Dan could not follow her. His mother had just signalled to him to help her prepare the tea. Frustrated, he watched through the window and, after a few minutes, he saw Selina walk with brisk strides across the terrace, through the Dutch garden and over to the glass-walled Orangery. There was Francis, still pacing restlessly. At any second he would learn that Dan had disobeyed his orders not to speak to Selina. Dan shrugged. What could Francis do, after all?

It was some time before he discovered. There was a boring interval of tea and conversation before he was able to bow to his mother and go off to construe his Latin. Mr Heron often set him an extra task to do before dinner, knowing that Dan enjoyed the work in the peaceful quiet of the library.

But today the library was not quiet. As soon as he pushed the door open, Dan realized that the room was not empty. Voices came from the alcove at the far end where he had left his books. Walking down the room, he saw Francis sitting on the table, swinging his legs, and Selina on a chair beside him.

'Why, Dan.' Selina sounded nervous. 'Come and see. Francis is teaching me to cut out paper flowers.'

Slowly, puzzled, Dan walked closer. He could see the white shapes of the flowers, scattered across the table and on the floor. They were regular and neatly cut out, but somehow awkward, as if the paper were too stiff for the task.

'Delightful, are they not?' Francis said.

Bending down, Dan picked one off the floor. It was half covered with print and, for a moment, he thought that they had been cutting up some old broadsheet. Then his eyes picked out a word or two and he looked up and saw the book on the table.

'What – what are you doing?'

'We told you,' Francis said. 'We are cutting out paper flowers.'

'But –' Dan whirled round to face Selina. 'Sal, you can't be letting him cut *that* up?'

Israel Ha –, – ackbeard, the letters, snipped into nonsense, swirled up at him from the confetti of paper and he snatched at them, foolishly, until his hands were full. And then saw how ridiculous it was. Opening his fingers, he let the paper drop in a slow shower to the floor. It was too late.

'Sal?' he said again.

Selina's face was hot and red and for a moment her bottom lip trembled. It was Francis who answered, his voice light.

'You see, little brother, Sally has grown up, as I told you. She has no more time for these childish games.' Deliberately, he pulled another page out of the pirate book and sliced into it with Selina's little, enamelled embroidery scissors. 'You should have been content to play by yourself.'

With as much dignity as he could manage, Dan said, 'Please give me the book.'

Selina picked it up and held it out. As her hands touched the worn leather binding, Dan thought she faltered briefly. Her eyes flicked down to look at it. But when she glanced up again Francis was watching her. He did not speak, but his eyes challenged. She spoke in a cheerful, bright voice. 'Here you are, Dan. Now run off and play. I'm sure you can find enough to do without bothering us.'

Almost choking, Dan walked down the room as steadily as he could, trying to ignore the limp that made him lopsided. As he turned to shut the door behind him, he saw the two of them standing at the end of the long, book-lined room. Selina glanced questioningly, almost appealingly, at Francis and he nodded back. A nod of satisfied approval.

Dan did not stop to think what it meant. As he closed the door, he felt himself start to shake. He did not think that he would cry. He had not cried since he was in petticoats. But he might not be able to stop himself screaming aloud with rage and grief.

A fine thing that would be. He could almost hear Francis's scornful comment. 'Tantrums? Dear, dear. Surely you are too old for those? But perhaps we should forgive your feebleness, because of your disability.' Biting hard on his lip, he walked blindly along the landing, clutching the mutilated book to his chest. But before he reached his bedroom he cannoned into something coming the other way.

'Forgive me, Master Daniel,' said a smooth voice. 'I did not realize you were in such a hurry.'

Looking up, Dan met the calculating stare of his eldest brother's secretary. Mr Ellerby held him by the arm and peered into his face.

'Indeed,' he said, 'you seem a little upset. Is there anything I can do to help you?' He looked a model of discreet, obliging family servant. Dan controlled his expression and tried to stare back as calmly.

'I am sorry I bumped into you. I have –' in his distracted state, he said the first thing that came into his head – 'I have an urgent message for the nurse. I was not looking where I was going.'

Mr Ellerby's face did not change. He still watched Dan shrewdly, almost as if he did not believe him. Dan stuck his head up and walked towards the upward staircase. As he started to climb the stairs, he saw that Mr Ellerby had not moved. He stood half-way along the landing, taking out his old brass snuffbox. Resignedly, Dan went up a few more steps.

As he did so, he saw a movement by the library door. Francis and Selina had come out arm in arm. They were not speaking, but Selina had an air of suppressed excitement and, as they started to go down the broad main staircase, she gave an involuntary skip.

And there, in the shadows of the landing, stood Mr Ellerby, quite still, with a pinch of snuff held to his nose. He was watching them all. Watching Dan go up and Francis and Selina go down. And on his face there was not the faintest clue to what he was thinking.

Chapter 7

COMING out of the nursery door on her way to fetch the dinner up, Betty almost fell over Dan. He was loitering on the top stair and, as she bounced out, she stumbled hard against him.

'Steady on!' She staggered.

He looked blankly at her, not seeming to understand what she was saying. White as death, with some old book clapped to his chest. Betty stared.

'What's amiss?'

'I –' He shook his head, dazed. 'Nothing. It's nothing.'

With an efficient hand, Betty pressed on his shoulder, making him sit on the top step. His knees gave at her touch and he slumped down.

'Proper faint-looking,' she said briskly. 'Do best to put your head atween your knees.'

'It's nothing, I tell you.' He was pale and stubborn. 'Leave me alone.'

Betty shook her head at him. 'Don't 'ee go choking it back, now. 'Twill make 'ee sick. Might as well tell.'

'I –' Suddenly he started to gabble, almost relieved to tell her. Load of old nonsense it was, too. All about paper flowers and that book he was carrying. If it weren't for his face, she would have laughed at him. But he was shaky enough to make her serious.

''Tes none so bad,' she said when he stuttered to a stop. 'The way you looked, I thought you'd seen Whispering Zak at least.'

Dan shook his head vaguely. 'No, I haven't been out of the park all day.'

'But you still could –' Betty stopped. 'Never told 'ee, did I?' she said softly.

'Told me? Told me what?' Colour was beginning to seep back into Dan's face and he looked at her sharply.

'Sick as you I was that day. Fair turned me up.' She shivered. 'Here in the park, he is. Playing hermit in that place in the wood. Miss Selina sent me.' She explained as quickly as she could, without describing the fear and horror she had felt. Less said about that the better. When she finished, Dan was icy calm.

'I was right, then. There is something frightful going on. Francis said it was just a game.'

Betty sniffed. 'That Zachary don't play games.'

Thumping an impatient fist on the stairs, Dan muttered, 'If only there were something we could do! If we knew something definite, we could decide what was best.' He looked up at Betty. 'You'll have to find out something. Now Sal thinks you're one of them, it should be possible.'

Betty looked back sulkily. 'Have to do what you say.' She glanced meaningfully at the nursery door and Dan went pink.

'I'm sorry. I shouldn't have said that about nurse. I was angry and upset. But I still need your help.'

He looked very thin and pale, sitting there in the shadows. Pathetic. What could he do, all alone, against Whispering Zak? Betty could have hit him for his frailness. He did not say anything else, but she felt as though he were hanging on her skirts, pleading. Good thing she was not soft, she told herself. She would not let him get round her. . . .

'Won't see nothing, stuck away up here,' she heard her voice say, 'but I'll keep my eyes open for 'ee. Need help from someone, you do.'

For the next two or three days, indeed, she saw less than usual. She was careful to avoid Selina and Francis, in case she should be sent on another errand to the hermitage.

But one night, as often, she was pulled out of her sleep by

thin, insistent wails. She had fallen asleep in the rocking chair, too tired to go to bed, and as she dragged herself to her feet she muttered rebelliously.

'When I be nurse, I'll have a rocker of my own. And her'll do all the night feeds. And I'll sleep and sleep and –'

She nodded longingly, but the baby gave a starving shriek and jerked her sickeningly awake. 'Little wretch!' She grabbed him from the crib and almost shook him. The fire was low and the only brightness came from a half moon, but she could have done the job with her eyes shut. Cradling the baby in one arm, she threw a clean linen cloth over her shoulder and lit a candle at the dying fire.

With the candlestick in her other hand, she padded down the stairs, rocking the baby to quiet its yells. It mumbled crossly, its bony little fists beating the air.

No use to knock on Lady Merrowby's bedroom door. Only a dig in the ribs would wake her. She lay in the middle of the big bed, her face relaxed for once as she slept. Betty put down the candlestick and administered the dig with a sharp finger.

'Your la'ship.'

Groggily, Lady Merrowby stirred among the pillows. As soon as she was properly awake, her face snapped into its usual controlled mask and she sat stiffly upright. 'Thank you, Betty. You may wait outside.'

With the door half open, Betty lingered for a while in the corridor. But after ten minutes or so she heard a soft noise. Bare feet tiptoeing along the landing. Having no wish to meet Sir Horatio in his nightcap, she stepped back inside the bedroom, leaving the door open a crack.

The footsteps moved cautiously nearer and paused a couple of doors away. Fingernails scratched on wood. Surreptitiously Betty opened her door a fraction wider and peered out. In the darkness the figure at Selina's door was only a black shape draped in a bedgown, but its height gave it away. Too tall for Sir Horatio. It was Francis.

'Sal.' His whisper was no more than a breath, but Betty strained her ears to catch it. 'Half an hour. I'll meet you down in the stables.'

That was all. Quickly, Betty jerked her head back and pulled the door to. The feet padded back along the landing.

'What are you doing, girl?' It was Lady Merrowby from behind her. 'You're distracting me, and the baby won't settle. I shall be awake all night. I told you to wait outside.'

'Sorry, your la'ship.' Betty slipped out, closing the door after her. She could feel her heart thumping. This was the trouble Dan had expected. It was ready to happen. Her instinct was to say nothing and keep safe, but she had promised to tell him. Surely it would do her no harm just to tell what she had heard? But it must be now. Nervously, she began to count the doors along the landing. Sir Horatio's. Selina's, tightly shut again. The next should be Dan's, but she dared not knock. Shivering a little, she eased the door open and crept across to the big, old-fashioned bed. It was heavily curtained. Pulling the curtain aside, she saw a dim, sleeping shape. Slowly, she reached out and touched it lightly on the cheek.

Dan stirred, flinging an arm out. Quickly, Betty clapped her hand over his mouth. 'Wake up,' she breathed. 'Wake up. Something's happening.'

He shook his head from under her hand and sat up. 'What – *Betty*?'

'Ssh! You'll raise the house.'

He spoke more softly. 'Whatever are you doing here?'

'There's something happening,' she said again. 'I've just heard Mr Francis talking to Miss Selina. Arranging to meet her in the stables in half an hour.'

'Oh, *that*.' Dan lay down again. 'I know all about that. They talked about it at dinner last night. They're going to Hightop Hill to see the sunrise.'

Betty shook at his shoulder. 'Long drive is it?'

'Only half an hour. Oh, do go away. I'm tired.'

She almost snorted. What could he know about being tired? But instead she said, very softly, ' 'Tes no more'n four o'clock.'

Dan pushed her away and scrambled out of bed. His legs sticking out of the bottom of his long white bedgown, he pattered across to peer at the clock on the mantelpiece. 'Quarter to four,' he whispered. 'What are they up to?'

'Sun doesn't rise till seven these mornings,' Betty said.

Dan scooped up a pile of clothes from a chair. 'If we hurry, we can be down there before them. Hide and listen to what they say.'

'Us both?' said Betty. 'But there's the babby. Got to take 'en upstairs when he's fed.'

Dan sat on the edge of the bed, pulling on his stockings. 'I'm scared of Whispering Zak too,' he said coldly, 'but I'm going. You go back to bed if you like.'

Betty threw up her head. 'Meet you down there,' she said sulkily as she flounced out.

She was only just in time. Lady Merrowby greeted her testily. 'I've been calling these five minutes.'

'Sorry, your la'ship. Must've fallen asleep.'

'A fine thing, for you to sleep when I'm waking.'

'Sorry.' Betty took the drowsy baby and, as Lady Merrowby settled down thankfully among her pillows again, hurried away up the stairs, the baby hiccuping contentedly against her chest.

'Don't 'ee cry now,' she muttered at it, 'or I'll have to stop up in the nursery and walk 'ee.'

She half hoped it would scream its head off. That would give her an excuse not to go down to the stable. But it was a contrary baby. As soon as she laid it in its cradle, it stuck a midget thumb into its mouth and fell fast asleep.

She would have to go. Or let Dan think he was braver than she was. Him! Pulling a shawl round her shoulders, she hurried soundlessly down the back stairs, with her shoes in her hand. Reaching the back kitchen door, she slipped them on and slid the bolts quietly, letting herself out into the stable yard.

The empty yard was full of moonlight. It caught the rounded tops of the cobbles palely, as if they were eggs. And, as carefully as if they had been eggs, Betty moved over them, keeping close to the wall and sliding round the sides of the buildings in case anyone should be watching.

At the stable door she paused. All the little, restless sounds of sleeping horses floated out to her. Tossing heads. Faint whickers. And the comforting stable smells. But no human sounds. She pushed the door open and stepped inside. Facing her was a row of stalls where dark shadows slept standing. At the end of the stalls was a larger space filled by a squat, bulky shape. Mr Ellerby's gig, its shafts propped up on a block. And, behind the gig, another shape.

''Tes no good,' Betty said in a quiet voice. 'You're clear as a crow in a snowfield.'

Dan wriggled out and stood up. 'It's hopeless,' he said crossly. 'There is nowhere at all to hide. If we go near the horses, they'll wake and give us away. And Sal and Francis will be here soon.'

Betty walked across and peered into the gig. 'Thought so,' she said briefly. ''Tes like the lace factor's gig. Great ugly boot it has.'

Without waiting for him to understand her, she climbed up into the gig, knelt down on the floor, facing the front, and wriggled herself backwards into the large empty space beneath the seat. The gig creaked loudly as she manœuvred, but in a couple of seconds her body was curled inside the clumsy, bulging boot and she was invisible, the cloth which covered the seat hanging down to hide her face.

'Come on.' Her bodiless whisper was eerie in the darkness. 'Room for two. Hop in quick, afore they come.' There was a pause while Dan wriggled, and then Betty said, 'And get your great boot out of my face.'

'Sorry. Can't see,' explained Dan. 'Not going backwards.' He suddenly sounded amused. 'A bit of squashing won't do your face any harm.'

She was so surprised that she did not reply for a moment. And then it was too late. She clutched at his arm as she heard a sound from the yard and his body, cramped up against hers, went tense. A single pair of feet tiptoed into the stable. There was a jangle of harness and a whinny from one of the horses. Then, almost inaudibly, the sound of someone whistling softly between his teeth.

The second pair of feet came more quickly, running softly across the cobbles. A skirt swished past the ends of the stalls and Selina's voice said breathlessly, 'I was as quick as I could be.'

'Ssh,' muttered Francis. 'If we can get away without rousing the boy, there'll be none to say we left at four instead of six.'

'And if we keep an eye to the sunrise, wherever we are,' whispered Selina eagerly, 'we shall be able to return with a fine description.'

Betty heard Francis chuckle. 'By sunrise, dear sister, you will be walking with your head sadly lowered. Unable to keep an eye to anything.'

'Sad,' Selina murmured with relish. 'I shall be as sad as never was. And near fainting? May I be near fainting, Francis?'

'Best to keep it in reserve,' said Francis sharply.

He's nervous. Betty, in her cramped hiding-place, caught the tension in his voice. Whatever they were off to do, it turned his courage. Not like Selina. She was lit up and ready to fire.

'Take your mare into the yard,' said Francis softly. 'Quiet as you can. We can't ride full out until we get fresh horses, and we must not be late.'

'Oh no,' Selina murmured gaily. 'It would not do to keep Mr Andrews of Taunton waiting for us.'

'It would not do to keep Zachary waiting,' Francis said. 'He's less patient. Come on.'

There was a low, clipping noise of hooves and a muffled curse from Francis as he banged against the shafts of the gig, sending a judder through it that made Betty bite her tongue. Then the cautious hooves on the cobbles. Then nothing. After three or four minutes, Dan raised his head.

'Well, we're none the wiser. Except that we know –'

'Hush up!' Betty poked at him and they crouched close again.

A very faint cough in the yard. And, even fainter, the sound of yet another pair of feet. She felt Dan move, as if he were about to speak, and she prodded him again. She would lose her place if she was found like this. Be sent home in disgrace.

The feet moved into the stable. There were soft horse noises. Little thuds. Jangles of harness. It was like listening to Francis all over again.

72

But then the gig jerked. Jerked once more. A horse stamped immediately in front of them. Then the gig leaned slightly sideways with the weight of someone climbing into it. Greatly daring, Betty lifted her head to look. Not six inches from her nose she saw a pair of lean calves covered with sober grey worsted stockings. A pair of feet in old, well-polished black shoes with discreet pewter buckles. There was a judder and the gig moved forwards. From her hiding-place, Betty could see nothing except the feet and legs and the inside of the gig, but she could guess well enough what had happened.

Mr Ellerby had harnessed a horse to his gig and was driving out of the stable yard. And she and Dan were trapped beneath his seat. Going – perhaps going towards Whispering Zak. The thought came suddenly, like a blow, and Betty pressed her trembling face against the floor of the gig, feeling sick with fright.

Chapter 8

As soon as Dan felt the gig move, he lifted his head slightly, ready to call out and stop it. But almost at the same moment he felt a sharp nip on his arm. Betty was pinching him urgently. He remembered that what would mean a scolding for him might mean dismissal for her. And not only that. If they were discovered, and it came to the ears of Zachary – Dan's throat started to prickle, as if the knife blade were already pressed tight against it. Very carefully, he lowered his head to the floor of the gig again and gritted his teeth. Wherever they were going, they would have to stay hidden and hope that nobody found them.

The horse pulled hard, feeling the extra weight, and Dan started to worry that it would betray them. Then he heard the whip crack and, a moment later, Mr Ellerby muttered, in a sleepy voice, 'Get on, Bessie. You've grown fat and lazy while I was abroad.'

He was too drowsy, Dan realized, to pay proper attention to their sluggish pace. Relaxing thankfully, he felt his head jar every time the wheels jolted on the uneven road, and reflected that it would have been unbearable if they had been travelling faster. As it was, he was shaken painfully, and red dust blew along the floor of the gig, grating in his nose and crunching between his teeth. But the further they went, the more important it seemed to stay concealed.

After about a quarter of an hour, it began to rain. The heavy drops pattered on the bulging back of the boot and splashed visibly round Mr Ellerby's shoes. The rain kept down the dust, but even sheltered as he was Dan felt his fingers and toes growing cold and numb, and he dared not move to ease them.

Mr Ellerby must have been equally uncomfortable, for after about an hour the gig drew up and they heard his voice shout, 'Ostler! Bring the fresh horse I ordered yesterday. Harness it up while I get a warm drink.'

The grumbling ostler and his boy set to work as Mr Ellerby disappeared.

'Gig be proper loaded up.' That was the ostler's boy. 'What've he got in there?'

The ostler sounded sharp and bad-tempered. 'Keep thy fingers out. Don't do to meddle with the likes of that one. Seen 'en before, I have.'

Quiet and still, Dan and Betty held their breath as the fresh horse was put between the shafts. Then, for a moment they were alone. Dan wriggled and Betty muttered sourly, 'A fine mess.'

'Ssh. He's coming back.'

There was a quick word and the sound of coins changing hands. This time their pace was faster. Clearly Mr Ellerby had less respect for the hired horse than he had for his own. From time to time, Dan dozed a little, but it was impossible to sleep much. His position was far too uncomfortable and his head was full of puzzled thoughts.

It seemed that Mr Ellerby must be following Francis and Selina, just as he had followed them to the British Lion. Otherwise it would be too much of a coincidence that he too should have set off in secret in the early morning. But why he should be following them and watching them Dan could not decide and the jolting of his head and the cramps in his body, squashed up close to Betty's, did not help him to think any more clearly.

Gradually, despite the heavy rain, the sky grew paler and in front of Dan's nose Mr Ellerby's legs became more and more clearly visible. At last there was a metallic rattle, as the horse's hooves clipped on cobble-stones, and they turned into what was clearly the yard of an inn, for Mr Ellerby shouted, 'Ostler!'

'Yessir!' The voice was brisk and quick to answer.

'Run my gig under cover and see to the horse. I may be gone some two or three hours. See that the horse is watered and ready to harness when I come back.'

'Yessir.'

All around them, feet were clattering and voices shouting in the early morning bustle. After a few moments they heard the unmistakable, precise tread of Mr Ellerby's feet walking away across the cobbles. Then a jangle of harness and stamping of hooves. And then the sounds grew muffled as the gig was pushed into some kind of shed.

'Dear Lord. Never been so dunched up in all my life,' muttered Betty. She began to crawl out without waiting for Dan to move. 'Must rub our arms and legs, or us'll be crippled worse than you ever were.'

She set to briskly, pummelling her limbs with hard little fists and Dan, moving in his turn, felt how painful it was. His feet were numb and frozen and his hands felt as lifeless as lumps of wood. They hurt as the blood flowed back into them.

'See here, I'll do it for 'ee!' Impatiently, Betty turned on him and began to knead his calves as if they were balls of dough.

'Get off!' Dan pushed her away and began to do it himself, less roughly. 'We must hurry.'

Betty stared at him. 'Why? Two or three hours, 'twill be. You heard 'en. A proper long wait. And I be famished.'

'Don't be silly,' Dan said, without looking up. 'We're not waiting here. We've got to follow Mr Ellerby and find out where he's gone.'

'And run ourselves into trouble, you mean.' Betty was furious. 'Got us here, and now you want to get our throats cut. You're mad.'

'What do you mean *I* got us here? It was your idea to hide in the gig.'

'You were the one was all for sneaking about and spying!'

'Look.' Dan breathed slowly and made himself calm. 'It will do us no good to quarrel. It may be dangerous, but we're here, and if we stay in the gig we are likely to be discovered. If we follow Mr Ellerby, at least we stand a chance of learning what's happening. And we shall not have put ourselves in danger for nothing.' Betty sniffed, but he ignored her. 'I shall go. You may do as you please.'

'Stop here without 'ee? And have 'ee call me a coward after?' Betty snorted, and bit her lip. 'No choice for me, is there?' She jumped off the gig and peered through the door. The yard was in a turmoil, with maids scurrying about, departing guests calling for their baggage, horses trampling and ostlers swearing. ''Tes no problem to sneak out. If you be set on it.'

'I am,' Dan said, with quiet determination.

Choosing their moment carefully, the two of them slid unobtrusively across the cobbles and out under the big arch into the street. It was a wide, bustling street, lined with shops, and all around people were stirring. A housewife opened a door and flung out some slops. A nightcapped head poked out through an upper window to sniff the air. Whatever town they had reached, it was waking up to a new day. Dan and Betty began to saunter down the road, unremarkable, shabby figures, grimy with red dust. Half-way down, an old man dozed on a chair, puffing at a pipe, but of Mr Ellerby there was no sign.

Dan pulled a face. 'Where should we go?'

'Got a handkerchief?' Betty said suddenly. 'A fine one, with a bit of lace to it?'

Dan fumbled in the pockets of his coat, jangling loose coins, and pulled out a small square of lawn with a fancy edging.

'Things are not bad enough for tears,' he said, with one of his queer flashes of humour. But Betty did not stop to smile. She snatched the handkerchief out of his hand and scampered off down the road towards the old man.

'Dear, oh dear.' Her voice floated back to Dan, all of a flutter. 'Gentleman's dropped his handkerchief. Did 'ee see 'en, granfer?'

Slowly the old man opened his eyes wider and took his pipe out of his mouth. 'Sees 'em all, I does,' he said peacefully. 'All ahurrying and ascurrying. Best off out here I be, with my daughter afretting round the kitchen. There bain't space nor chair for a body to call his own.'

'Did 'ee see the gentleman, then?' Betty repeated eagerly. 'Small he was, in a plain coat and a bag-wig, with a back like a poker.'

'Course I saw 'en,' muttered the old man. Dan sauntered closer to catch his words. But the toothless mouth creased into a cunning smile. 'Thee doesn't want to go achasing 'en, my maid. 'Tes a fine handkercher, but the likes of he do have aplenty such. What's to stop 'ee walking off up to old Mother Naylor's and selling 'en?'

Betty drew herself up primly. 'My mother brought me up honest,' she said. 'And besides –' her face turned as cunning as his – 'a gentleman like that might reward a poor girl as is too honest to mouch his handkerchief. He'll likely give more than old Mother Naylor.'

'Not he, my dear. Tight-fisted, that one, I could tell.' The old man closed his eyes again, and Betty almost stamped her foot with impatience.

'Please tell. Where did he go?'

Wearily the old eyes opened once more. 'Why, down there, wench. Down towards the river.' He waved a hand. 'But old Mother Naylor's –'

He was still rambling on while Betty darted away down the hill. Dan caught her up near the corner, but there was still no sign of Mr Ellerby as they looked along the road.

'Could be anywhere,' Betty said dispiritedly. 'Us won't do no good walking round and round the town. A proper big place it be, too. And I be starved to a bone.'

'I think we must be in Exeter,' Dan said thoughtfully. 'We were over two hours on the road, going south. And there's a river. And that must be the city wall down there.' He glanced up the slope behind them and then back at Betty who was frowning bad-temperedly. 'Wait a moment.'

There was a small, dingy baker's across the road. He ran in, pulling a coin out of his pocket, and bought a loaf of bread. Once she had a bit of it in her hand to munch, Betty cheered marvellously.

'I was never in such a big place afore,' she said. 'They do say as there be a great church in Exeter, big enough to swallow all

78

the houses in our village. I'd love to tell 'em –'

'You can't tell anyone,' Dan said vaguely, looking up and down the road that ran along the wall. 'Do you want people to know that you have been here? Besides, we are not going that way. It looks as though we are walking out of the city.' He bit hugely at his piece of bread and, as he did so, a procession of coaches came down a road further along, moving down the slope and turning away from them.

There was no mistaking the purpose of the procession. The first vehicle was low and flat and painted with shiny black paint, an empty hearse, moving with ponderous dignity. It swung out and round the corner and, automatically, Dan and Betty bowed their heads, although there was no coffin. Behind the hearse came two coaches, one after the other. Their windows were heavily shuttered and the coachmen drove with solemn faces. The coachmen –

With a sudden snap of terror, Dan recognized a face. The last coachman, gaunt as Death himself, wore no wig, but his own long grey hair, tied back into a neat tail. Hair that usually hung lank and coarse around the bony face. Dan stooped forward and shrank back into a doorway. 'Look down, Betty,' he hissed. 'Lower.'

Puzzled, she obeyed and when the coaches had pulled away along the road, Dan tugged at her sleeve. 'Come on. We must follow. But don't let them see you. Not for a second.'

'Follow them?' Betty frowned. 'Us was following that Mr Ellerby.'

'Didn't you recognize him?' Dan gulped. 'Whispering Zak was on the box of that last coach.'

'Dear Lord!' Betty went suddenly white. 'Us'd do best to go back and hide.'

'We go on,' Dan said grimly. 'They can't harm us if they don't see us.'

It was easy to follow the coaches. They were travelling at no more than a walking pace and the coachmen did not gaze about. After a few yards, the road turned round the corner of a building, the horses' hooves striking sharply on stones, and the procession drew on to the wide expanse of a wharf. Dan dragged Betty back into the shadow of the building and the two of them looked cautiously along the quay.

The broad grey stretch of river gleamed dully in the early morning light, faint wisps of mist still floating over its surface. There was little to disturb it this morning. A few boats were moored down at the far end and a sailing ship, of no great size, was tied up nearer. Dan could just read her name at the distance. The *Rose of Barnstaple*. Her reflection, pale as a cloud, floated upside down at her water-line. The quay itself seemed empty except for a few men lounging about looking for work and a couple of boys crouched playing marbles.

Slowly, the coaches ground along the waterside until they drew level with the *Rose of Barnstaple* and stopped. For a moment it seemed that nothing was going to happen. Then, with grave dignity, a tall figure climbed from the first coach and began to walk across to the ship. His large black hat hid the shape of his head and the thick folds of his mourning cloak were gathered loosely round his body. Standing beside the ship, he shouted a few inaudible words to the seamen on her deck.

''Tes no good,' Betty said nervously. 'Us'll learn nothing here. Oh Dan, come back to the gig.'

'Ssh.' Dan pulled her closer. 'We're in the right place for sure. It's not just Zachary. Look at the corner of that lane along there. He's hidden now, but if you watch you'll see him peep out.'

Sure enough, a moment or two later a neat, dark head peered round the corner further down the quay. Mr Ellerby was lounging there casually, as if he had been out walking and had paused to observe the unusual sight of a funeral procession on the wharf. But he was taking good care not to be seen by the mourners.

'Whispering Zak *and* that Ellerby,' Betty muttered. Dan felt her shoulder, pressed against his, tremble slightly. 'Don't mean no good.'

The tall black figure by the ship now made an impatient beckoning gesture and one of the boys came running from his game of marbles. Dan saw a coin change hands and the boy nodded eagerly. Then he set off along the quay towards them at a jogtrot. The tall man turned back to his coach and, as he turned, Dan caught sight of his face.

It was Francis.

Betty gasped softly. Dan, greatly daring, reached out an arm. The boy with the message had drawn almost level with them and his trot slowed to a walk as he bit his coin. Dan touched his shoulder and spoke, trying to sound idly curious.

'What's afoot, then? A hearse on the quay? And so early?'

The boy grinned. 'Come in last night, her did. The *Rose of Barnstaple*. Too late to unload. Customs house be all locked up.' He gestured at the building beside them. 'I be sent for the Customs Officer.' He chuckled. 'Mortal pleased he'll be, to be dragged out of bed. He was drinking with my dad till nigh on three.'

'They'd do best to wait a bit?' Betty said innocently.

'Could be they're afeard the sun will get up.' The boy grinned gruesomely. 'Proper grand gent he be, as spoke to me. Couldn't stand the stink.'

'Stink of what?' Dan was too quick, too curious, but the boy did not notice.

'Why, the body,' he said with relish. ''Tes the body they be come for. That's my message, see. *Tell the Customs Officer that Mrs Andrews of Taunton has come for her husband's coffin.*'

He pranced away, full of glee at the thought of the rotting flesh on board. Betty pulled a squeamish face.

'There 'tes,' she said. 'They be come to join in the funeral party. 'Tes no great mystery. Us'll be best off going back to the gig.'

'But Francis and Sal don't know anyone called Andrews of Taunton.' Dan was puzzled. 'And why the secrecy? And why Whispering Zak? No, wait a while. Let's see what happens.'

Nothing at all happened for quite some time. Clearly the Customs Officer was dressing and breakfasting before he condescended to appear. The line of black vehicles stayed motionless on the quay and the *Rose of Barnstaple* was equally motionless on the river, only its reflection stirring gently as a breeze rippled the surface of the water.

At last, with a clattering of shoes on stones, a portly figure appeared round the bend in the street. His eyelids were puffed and a scar on his chin showed that he had shaved hastily. He strode along self-importantly and beside him hurried a tall, pimply young man, with a brown wig and startlingly red eyebrows.

'B-be calm, uncle. There is no need for such a p-p-pace.'

'The business of the port,' muttered the stout man pompously. 'Exeter is a great port, nephew. You do not realize, knowing only Lyme. That is nothing but a broken down village.'

'Everyone knows the p-p-port of Exeter is decayed,' hissed the spotty young man rebelliously as he followed on to the quay.

It was Francis who climbed from the coach to meet them and, even from a distance, it was clear that the Customs Officer was disposed to be difficult. His head jerked impatiently and he made irritated gestures towards the *Rose of Barnstaple*.

All at once, Francis held out a languid hand to open the door of the first coach. With a care that was almost tenderness, he handed out a lady from inside.

''Tes her,' Betty said softly. ''Tes the poor widow.'

Heavily clad in mourning and shrouded in a veil that fell over her face and down on to her chest, a frail figure stepped from the coach. As she came down the step, she stumbled weakly and would have fallen were it not for Francis's steadying arm.

The Customs Officer stopped bristling and took off his hat respectfully. His nephew bowed low, with a clumsy attempt at polite gallantry, obviously impressed. There was something at once pathetic and brave about the slender young widow, standing there in the cold November morning. Her maid, climbing down behind her, was coarse and heavy, a barrel of a woman with a handkerchief held ostentatiously to her eyes, but Mrs Andrews looked as though only strength of will kept her on her feet.

Gently, she put a black-gloved hand on the Customs

Officer's arm. Then, as if to plead more eloquently, she flung back her veil with a graceful gesture and fixed her large, sorrowful eyes on his puffy face.

'God!' said Dan.

'Her's weeping, too,' Betty murmured admiringly. 'Real tears. You'd swear her'd lost the best husband in the world.' With a grin she looked at Selina's face, piteously sobbing under Mrs Andrews's veil.

It was clear that the Customs Officer was deeply affected by the grief of the delicate widow. He gave a brisk nod and signalled to the ship with a wave of his hand. There was a quick flurry of sailors on her deck and a coffin was carried slowly and reverently down the gangplank. Men climbed from the second coach to take it on their shoulders. They paced with it towards the hearse and, all the while, the widow, with her veil lowered once more, swayed as if she were near fainting. Once she made a slight move as if to go to the coffin, but her maid caught at her arm and the long box was slid gently on to the back of the hearse.

Dan watched it all, knowing it was as false as a play, but moved, in spite of that, by the brave uprightness of the widow as she climbed back into her coach. He was jerked back to consciousness again by Betty shaking at his shoulder.

'Quick!' she muttered. 'They be whipping up the horses. When they turn, Zachary'll see us for sure.'

As if she could not stop herself, she spun away in panic, ready to run off up the road. Dan caught at her arm. Behind him he could hear the slow crunch of the big wheels as the gloomy cavalcade moved round, ready for its journey back.

'I can't run fast enough,' he whispered desperately. 'Not with my leg.'

For an instant, Betty looked horrified. Then she became suddenly brisk. 'I'm a fool,' she muttered. 'Zachary'll look round for sure if he hears running feet. Quick. Behind the Custom House.'

With a fiercely efficient hand, she propelled Dan along until the two of them were shielded by a corner of the brickwork. They huddled there, shaking in the shadows, and listened to the noise of the hearse and the black coaches rolling heavily by, on and on.

When at last the sound died away, Betty relaxed, with a rueful grin. 'Thought us was done that time, for sure.'

'We're not safe yet,' said Dan. 'We must get back to the gig, before Mr Ellerby sees us. Come on.'

They crept quickly along the road, keeping to the shadows of the buildings and looking nervously over their shoulders, expecting to see Mr Ellerby's dark figure appear at any moment. As they rounded the corner, to take the road up the hill, a voice at their elbows surprised them.

'Found 'en, did 'ee? Bet he never gave 'ee a penny.' The old man was still sitting in the doorway, watching the world through half-closed eyes. Betty forced Dan to a walk.

'Never found 'en,' she said cheekily. 'I'll lay as thee told us wrong, granfer.'

'Said 'ee'd do best to keep it.' The old man winked knowingly.

With what seemed unbearable slowness, they walked away from him and up to the inn yard. It was not quite as busy as before and, trembling with impatience, they had to wait for a moment when the ostlers' backs were turned.

'He'll be here afore we be safe,' Betty was muttering. 'He'll be here for sure.'

But Mr Ellerby did not come and, in a few moments, they were crawling back into their uncomfortable hiding-place in the gig.

Dan was frowning. 'It makes no sense. A funeral? Was it all some kind of game?'

'Told 'ee before,' Betty said shortly. 'That Zachary don't have no time for games. No, 'tes plain as day what they were at.' She giggled suddenly. 'Taking a box that size through the Customs unopened? Right past the Customs Officer's nose? Might make no sense to 'ee, but it makes money-sense to Whispering Zak.'

'Smuggling?' All at once, Dan felt sick. 'But that's dangerous.' The chill he felt had nothing to do with the cold boards underneath him.

84

'Good luck to 'em, I say.' Betty was still chuckling. 'Must've been a proper weight, a box like that full of brandy casks. Or maybe 'twas tea.' She shifted uncomfortably. 'Have 'ee got more bread?'

Silently, Dan handed her a piece. But he could not eat. He stared at the dirty floor of the gig. Prison or transportation. That was what Sal and Francis were risking. That was why Sal had been so excited in the dark stable that morning. He leaned his head on the boards in such misery that, even when the horse was put to the gig and Mr Ellerby climbed in to drive away, he hardly noticed anything.

'So.' The man in the brown coat watched, smiling faintly, as the newcomer took off his travelling cloak and sat down at the inn table. 'It went well?'

'It was as you planned it.' The man in the black coat nodded reminiscently as he took a folded paper from his pocket. 'A neat landing, with a widow as grief-struck as you could wish to see.'

'And no suspicion?'

'Not a tremor.'

The man who called himself James Prior gave a complacent smile and then sat forwards briskly. 'Very good. And now we wait for the second landing. At Lyme. It is arranged?'

The other man nodded, but frowning. 'Indeed – but is it not too great a risk? So soon?'

'Risk?' The man in the brown coat raised his eyebrows. 'I pay them to take risks.'

'But to put yourself in danger by too great haste –'

'Listen!' A fist thumped the table. 'It is not in haste *my* danger lies, but in delay. All the while I linger on this coast, Zachary will endeavour to track me down and discover me. He hates and fears me, and he is not a man to be despised. That is why I have planned for a second quick operation. The odds in favour of success will not be as good as the first time – but they will be good enough for me. I shall make a fine sum of money and then leave France, and danger, behind me.'

'And if the second landing fails? And they are taken?'

'Then at least they will not be able to betray me. They will have had no time to learn anything – undesirable.'

'But you are risking their lives, sir.'

The man in the brown coat shrugged indifferently. 'I pay them, as I said.' Reaching across, he took the folded paper from between his companion's fingers. Opening it, he read, with a satisfied smile, and then folded it again, sliding it into his pocket.

It was a letter from his London banker, informing him that a substantial sum of money had recently been deposited to the credit of his account.

Chapter 9

*B*ETTY was still grinning to herself as she hurried up the back stairs. All through the long, uncomfortable journey home she had been imagining the solemn, pompous Customs Officer letting the great box of tea – surely it had been tea? – slide unopened past his nose. And Selina, as cool as ice, tricking him with her false tears. It was a good joke.

But when she reached the nursery door her amusement stopped abruptly. There would be trouble. Aunt Annie would be enraged, wanting to know where she had been. Perhaps the whole household had been searching for her. Shivering slightly, Betty pushed the door open.

It was one of the nurse's good days. The nursery was clean and orderly and her cap and apron were fresh and neat. But that only made it worse. She was furious. As Betty came in, she glared round at her.

'Back again? Where've 'ee bin all morning? Leaving me all the work, and never a word. A fine carry-on!'

'I'm sorry,' Betty said meekly.

'Well then? Where's thee bin?'

Betty swallowed. The shadow of Whispering Zak swelled huge in her mind. 'I can't tell 'ee, aunt. But 'twas nothing wrong I did. I promise.'

'And I'm to rest content with that?' The nurse tapped a finger on the wooden arm of her chair. 'Send 'ee packing, that's what I should do. Back to thy mother.'

'Yes, aunt.' Betty lowered her eyes. It was what she had feared. To be turned off in disgrace, sent away in the carrier's cart with her little wooden box. And her mother struck with grief. But she dared not say any more. She stood staring at her feet, waiting for the order to go and pack.

But the old nurse coughed awkwardly. ''Twould break thy mother's heart,' she muttered. 'Poor Mary. The first babby I ever nursed, her was, when I was not so big as thee. Mother was ailing then, and I had Mary from a week old. 'Twould break her down to see 'ee come back in trouble.'

Betty looked up, but her aunt's eyes slid away quickly, not meeting her glance.

''Tes best I have a rocker. And kinfolks be most comfortable. So – well, I've not told of 'ee. There's no one knows as thee wasn't here all morning. I kept it quiet. For thy mother's sake, mind.'

It was not the real reason, and they both knew it. As things were, the old nurse could not manage by herself. And to bring a stranger in would be to court trouble. A stranger would not understand how things were. Betty realized how much her aunt needed her. But it could not be said aloud.

'Thankee, aunt,' she said mildly.

The knobby hand relaxed on the chair arm. 'Thee's not to go unpunished, mind. Even if thee did no wrong away, 'twas wrong to *be* away. There's all the mending in the big press. Thee can start now.'

Betty did not argue, but she sighed. She knew that heap of mending. Things so old they would be better thrown away. Hours and hours of pointless work. She went across to the press and began to sort through the pieces of old cloth.

'That's a good wench. Us'll say no more about it, then?'

Betty looked up to nod, and the nurse's face grew patchily red with embarrassment. To break the tension, Betty said briskly, 'I'll make the fire up. Us'll feel better with a good blaze.'

She knelt down, making a busy, cheerful clatter with the fire irons. Such a clatter that she did not hear the light footsteps outside. She jumped with surprise when Selina burst into the room, her skirts swirling.

'Nurse, darling, you *will* do this for me, won't you?' Selina's voice was spikily gay. 'Everyone else is too busy, and you know how bad my sewing is. I should make a pig's ear of it.'

Betty did not look round. The memory of Mrs Andrews of Taunton, weak with grief, was still too strong. If she glanced at Selina, she might giggle.

'What've 'ee got there, my duck?' The nurse's voice was indulgent. Selina had always been her favourite.

'A present from Francis. Aren't they lovely? I want to wear them tonight, so you will sew them on for me, won't you, nurse dear?'

Her voice was a trifle too quick, too glib, and Betty looked over her shoulder automatically. And saw what Selina was holding. At once, all her longing to giggle vanished completely.

'Our Betty'll do 'em,' the nurse was saying. 'Her's got clever fingers. Here, Betty.'

Slowly, Betty straightened and walked across the room, her eyes fixed on Selina's hands, on the long strips which hung from them, pale as cream, delicate as thistledown. It must be a mistake, she was thinking. Yet she had seen those patterns in a pattern book. And once the lace factor had had a piece. A chilly air seemed to creep round her as she went towards Selina.

'Queer he didn't give 'em to 'ee straight off,' the nurse said casually. 'Fine set of lace flounces like that. Fancy waiting.'

'Oh, you know what a tease he is, nurse. He said he wanted to be sure I deserved them.' Selina spoke lightly, but her eyes flickered. Betty went on staring at the lace. She was not taken in. Those flounces had never come out of Francis's travelling-bag. She knew where they had come from, as clear as if she had seen them lifted from the box. They had come in a big bundle, big and heavy as a body, and worth a fortune, if anyone could get it through the Customs.

'You will do them for me, won't you, Betty?' Selina held them out, but Betty drew her hands back.

'I'd best wash first, miss. From doing the fire. The lace marks easy.'

'Betty knows,' the nurse said proudly. 'Best little lacemaker round Honiton way, her was. Gave me her first piece of trolley lace. Fan pattern, proper neatly done. I'll show 'ee.'

As she poured the water from the ewer into the big bowl, Betty could hear her aunt shuffling round the room, searching in cupboards. But the noises seemed far away. She stared down at her own thin face, reflected in the smooth circle of water. A grim face. Grim as her mother's when she counted out the coins the lace factor had given her. They clinked dully, making a poor, small heap on the kitchen table. No more than three quarters of what she had expected. And the lace factor's voice saying silkily, 'It's still the French lace takes the cream of the market, Mrs Pinney. In spite of all the laws. There's such a call for it that we have to buy it first when we can get it.'

All the heaps of coins on all the tables round Honiton way would be small, this month and months after.

Drying her hands on the linen towel, Betty turned. 'There, miss. I'll do 'em now.' She held her voice steady, but she could not resist a probing question as she took the flounces. 'Fine pieces, miss. Chantilly? Out of France?'

'Oh, Betty!' Selina gave a brittle laugh, but her eyes frowned a warning. 'Would Francis give me an illegal present?'

'Of course not, miss.' With her other hand, Betty took the long-sleeved stay bodice that Selina was holding. 'I'll take off the old ruffles, then? And sew on the new?'

'Yes, please. Before dinner. And Betty –' Selina hesitated, choosing her words. 'When you have finished, bring them down to my room yourself. I shall be happy to reward you.'

She swirled away, and Betty fetched a needle and thread and went to sit on the window seat where the light was good. She could not help feeling a reluctant pleasure as she spread the new flounces. Beautiful work, it was. Finer than anything she had ever seen. But when she stuck the needle carefully through the edge, it was as though she stuck it into her mother's flesh.

It was not a long task. In half an hour, she had finished and she slipped down the back stairs and along the landing to Selina's bedroom, knocking discreetly.

'Come in.' Selina was standing by the bed in her long linen chemise, picking at the bed curtains. 'Oh, Betty, it's you.

You've finished?' She was breathing fast, and her face was paler than usual.

'Yes, miss.' Puzzled, Betty shut the door and went across to the bed. She had expected to find Selina wild with glee at the success of her precious game. Why did she look so nervous?

'Help me on with the stays,' Selina said quickly. 'I want to talk to you. You must have guessed that that was why I asked you to come down.'

Betty helped her slip her arms into the sleeves and then pulled on the stay-laces to tighten them. Her hands were shaking, but all Selina said was, 'Your fingers are cold.'

'Sorry, miss.'

'Now the petticoats. Then the dress.'

The petticoats tied at the waist, the top one, which showed under the dress, finely quilted and embroidered. Over them, the dress slipped on like a coat, and the lace ruffles had to be eased through the narrow sleeves and fluffed out to hang elegantly at the elbows. Betty smoothed them, although she longed to rip them away, and then fastened the dress down to the waist.

'There,' said Selina shakily, waving her arms, 'Aren't they beautiful? You were wrong when you said they came from Chantilly. Zachary said they were made in Bayeux.'

'Chantilly they call 'em still, miss. 'Tes the pattern.' Betty spoke stiffly. She could not bring herself to praise the lace. Instead, she sniffed and said, 'Worth it all, was it then?'

'I – oh, Betty!' Suddenly, unexpectedly, Selina sat on the bed and hid her face in her hands.

'What's amiss?' Betty was astounded. 'Went well, didn't it?'

'It went marvellously. Just as I had imagined.' For a moment Selina smiled. Then her face turned dull, almost afraid. 'But I thought it would be only once. For the fun of it. Now Zachary says –' She looked down at her feet in their ornate silk shoes. 'He says we must do it again. *Next week*. It's madness. I told him so, but –' She looked up again and her face was white. 'He is a very frightening man, isn't he?'

Betty snorted. 'You could say smallpox is uncomfortable!

'Twould be as far short. But you said 'twas the best game ever. You're not pleased to do it again?'

'It is too soon!' Selina thumped the bedclothes. 'Too soon and too near the same place. Lyme Regis is where he has chosen next. I argued, and I could see Francis agreed with me, but he would not say so.' She clenched her hands together, and Betty could see them shaking. 'You will think me a fool, I know, but I had thought Francis planned it all. I thought Zachary was working for *him*.'

'And now you've found,' Betty said softly, 'as 'tes the other way about. And Whispering Zak has you in his grasp. 'Twas always his way. 'Twould take something wonderful to make 'en work for another, miss.'

'He's like some foul sea monster!' Fear and disgust mingled in Selina's face. 'Black and hideous. Drawing everyone in unsuspecting.' She screwed her eyes up and then opened them wide, as if another thought had struck her. 'But you won't tell him? You won't tell him what I said?'

'Me?' Betty laughed shortly. 'Think I'd seek 'en out when there's no cause? Hope I never see 'en again.'

'But you're bound to.' Selina looked up in surprise. 'He has not told you?'

'Told me what?' Betty felt the whole surface of her skin begin to prickle.

'You are a part of the next plan. Francis and I cannot go as far as Lyme in secret. We need an excuse to travel that way. And you are to be the excuse.'

'Me?' Feeling as though all her bones had dissolved, Betty forgot her manners and sat down abruptly on the bed.

'It is a clever scheme. These are Zachary's instructions.' Selina's mouth twisted wryly. 'You must be homesick. Pale and refusing to eat, pining for a sight of your family. And Francis, on a whim, will propose that we two take you home for a visit. That will give us an excuse to travel past Honiton, and that takes us the best part of the way to Lyme. We can set off early and be back by nine or ten at night, with no one any the wiser.'

Betty stared down at her fingers, unable to speak. How had she found herself in this position? To be asked to aid the smuggling that would rob her own people of their just wages! Now she knew why Zachary had looked at her in such scorn when he heard that she came from near Honiton.

'We shall not stop at your village, of course,' Selina went on, unaware of Betty's thoughts. 'But there is still a place for you in the plan. Has Zachary ever described to you how it is done? With the funeral?' Betty nodded. 'Well, that – that *woman* they found for my maid in Exeter would not deceive a child. It was risking all our necks to use her. No respectable family would employ such a person. I tell you, I was in a sweat of fear all the time in case the Customs Officer came close enough to smell her breath.'

And her so cool and playing the widow so perfectly. Betty could have admired her. If it had only been tea in the coffin.

'So you are to be the maid,' Selina said cheerfully. 'Dressed properly, with your hair in a knot, you will pass inspection.'

Betty was outraged. Her heart thudded in her chest. But to protest would have betrayed everything. And a thought slid suddenly into her mind. If she were with them, she could seek an opportunity to put an end to this lace smuggling for ever. They might find that they had carried their destruction with them.

'Very good, miss,' she said meekly.

Selina stood up. 'Now you must go back, before nurse wonders what you are at. Here.' She held out a small coin. 'In case she asks. There will be much more to come to you when next week's work is over.'

Betty took the coin reluctantly and went across to the door. But as she opened it there was a footstep outside and she drew back automatically and closed it again. Selina smiled palely.

'Yes, that's how I feel, too. But you need not be afraid. There's no spy. That will be Thomas, bringing up Dan's dinner on a tray.'

'He's ill?' Betty was surprised. When she left him, he had been gloomy, but not ailing.

'Ill?' Selina laughed. 'Where have you been all day? Surely you didn't miss the hue and cry for him?'

'No – no, of course not,' Betty said, with guilty quickness.

'My father said that if he chose to go fishing when he should be at his books, he should spend three days shut in his room. To work without distraction.'

Poor Dan. Without distraction. Betty could have smiled. His thoughts would be distraction enough. She heard Thomas's footsteps passing on the way back and reached for the door handle.

'Wait.' Selina came quickly across the room. 'There was something else I wanted to say. Since we must undertake this second funeral, I am glad you are in the plan. At least there is someone I can trust, who will not laugh at my fears.'

Smiling, she held her hand out and, for an instant, Betty faltered. Those brown eyes were so trusting. Poor Miss Selina. She meant no harm. How could she understand, living as she did, the meaning of what she had done? It was all Betty could do to reach out her hand in reply.

Then, behind Selina's hand, she saw the Chantilly lace ruffles swinging at the elbow and her sympathy vanished. With false frankness, she shook the hand firmly. 'You can trust me, miss.'

Letting herself out, she shut the door and paused outside Dan's room, trying the handle cautiously. But the door was locked. Oddly relieved, she clattered away up the stairs.

The pile of mending was still waiting and she sat down by the fire with it. Threading her needle, she began to sew, watching the flames flicker in the fireplace and the shadows grow longer and darker.

Hours afterwards, when the nurse and the baby were both asleep, Betty was still by the fire, screwing her eyes up to see the stitches in the dim light. The fire was low, and the windows were black with the night outside, but the upright figure by the hearth did not move except for the quick flash of the fingers which took the needle backwards and forwards, a red gleam from the fire catching it every now and again. The moon rose and shone whitely, but the face it glanced on gave no sign of the turbulent thoughts that moved behind it. Pink in the firelight, Betty sat with a stern, set face, and there was no break in the steady movement of her needle to and fro.

Chapter 10

DAN saw the door handle turn as Betty loitered outside, but he did not take any notice of it. All through the next three days it turned. Sometimes someone came in. Sometimes nobody did. By the end of the third day, he did not care any more. His thoughts kept him too busy.

The punishment itself did not trouble him. His father had been furious, losing his usual elegant calmness, but only because he thought Dan had played truant to go off with the village boys. It would have been an amusing mistake if the truth were not so serious. Silently, Dan had let the mistake stand and had accepted the punishment. He was even glad of the huge pile of work that Mr Heron had set him. At least it served as a distraction.

But by the end of the third day, with the Latin and mathematics long since done, he began to find concentration impossible. Dully he stared down at the list of the bays and capes of France which he had been given to learn. *Baie de la Somme, Baie de la Seine, Golfe de St Malo.* . . . As he read each name, he remembered the *Rose of Barnstaple* bobbing at the Exeter quayside. She had come from that coast no doubt, beating across the Channel from some French port. Dieppe? Le Havre? Cherbourg? Cherbourg was the nearest. She had slipped across the Channel and bided her time, waiting to sail up the Exeter canal and into the river to berth at the right moment, the night before the hearse came. It had all been so meticulously planned.

But at least that part of it was over. Wrong or right, it was successfully accomplished and Sal and Francis were safely back home. What made Dan frown and chew his nails was the memory of Mr Ellerby, following to the British Lion and lurking hidden on the Exeter quay. What was his interest in it all? Idly, Dan began to draw the shape of the north French coast.

Unless – the pen nib dug into the paper, suddenly spattering ink. Unless Mr Ellerby were a government agent, investigating for the customs service. It seemed a fantastic idea, and yet –

Restlessly, Dan got up and began to pace the room. It could be true. And if it were, Selina was still in terrible danger. If only there were some way he could warn her! Leaning across the table, he flung the window open, peering out into the garden, to see if there were anyone who might take a message.

But the day was grey and dark. Black clouds were bringing an early twilight and the plants in the formal garden, orderly in their straight rows, whipped backwards and forwards, buffeted by the wind. It was no day for pleasant strolling. Even while he was looking, it started to rain, and the wind drove fat droplets through the open window to splash messily across Mr Heron's neatly written lists.

Dan slept badly that night. His dreams were about nothing more serious than fishing, but they were charged with an almost unbearable sense of doom and danger, and through them all slid the secretive, black-coated figure of Mr Ellerby, never clearly seen, but always peering from behind some corner. Towards dawn, exhausted, Dan fell at last into a deeper sleep.

'Daniel.' The voice which woke him was gentle and unreproachful. Opening his eyes, he saw Mr Heron standing by the bed.

'Good morning, sir.' Scrambling out of bed, Dan stood shivering in his nightshirt.

'I have come to release you,' Mr Heron said gravely. 'But first, I regret to say, Sir Horatio has charged me to give you a beating.'

'Oh.' Dan looked down. 'Is he still angry?'

Mr Heron's mouth twitched. 'He spoke of the need for you to appreciate your responsibilities. But I imagine that he himself preferred fishing to Latin when he was a boy.'

96

'It's not that,' Dan said. 'When he was twelve, although you might not think it now, he could thrash any boy in the village. What he doesn't like is that I'm so – so much smaller and feebler than most of them.'

Looking at him almost pityingly, Mr Heron picked up his heavy ruler. 'Hold out your hand.'

'I don't think,' said Dan honestly, 'that that was the sort of beating my father had in mind.'

Mr Heron pressed his lips together. 'Well, it's the only sort of beating I am prepared to give.' He looked down at Dan's outstretched palm and winced. 'No, not your right hand.'

Changing hands, Dan stood biting his lip and waiting for the ruler to fall. He could not look at his tutor's stoical face. He knew that Mr Heron was outraging all his own principles of civilized behaviour between gentlemen. Nevertheless, the blows were hard. Six of them stung down on to the tender flesh of Dan's palm and he bit his lip harder to keep himself from crying out.

'There.' Mr Heron put the ruler down with an expression of distaste. 'I think we may now consider the matter closed. We shall resume lessons as usual after breakfast.'

'Sir,' Dan said suddenly, 'I wasn't really fishing. You know that I would rather do Latin than go fishing any day.'

'Unnatural boy.' The tutor smiled. 'I will confess that I was a little puzzled. But you are not going to tell me what you *were* doing?'

'I don't think I can. But can I ask you something?'

Gravely, Mr Heron nodded.

'If you knew,' Dan clenched his fists, 'that someone close to you was doing something wrong, and was in danger, what would you do?'

The tutor frowned. 'I suppose,' he said slowly, 'that I should at least point out the wrong and warn of the danger. Then I should have to settle in my own mind whether I was bound to inform someone in authority.' His eyes were worried. 'Are you sure you can't tell me about it?'

Dan shook his head awkwardly. 'But I promise you that *I* have done nothing wrong.'

Ill at ease, the tutor nodded and went towards the door. 'If I can help you at any time,' he murmured, 'be assured that I will. And I shall expect you in the library after breakfast.'

As he closed the door, Dan started to dress, wondering when he would be able to talk to Selina. It was not long before he saw her. When he went down to the breakfast room, she was sitting at the table, toying with a piece of toast. But she was not alone. Francis and Sir Horatio were there as well, deep in conversation.

'Quixotic, my dear Francis,' Sir Horatio was saying. 'Positively quixotic. I told you so at first, and my opinion has not changed. Nothing would induce me to rise before ten o'clock. I could not have done it even to view a sunrise as you and Selina did. And what a worthless expedition that was!'

'Such rain!' Selina said mischievously. 'It was a most exhilarating journey.'

'And now this scheme.' Sir Horatio shook his head. 'And for a mere servant girl. I think you are lunatic.'

Dan sat down beside Selina and took a piece of toast, buttering it as he listened idly to Francis's reply.

'As I told you before, Father, the girl herself is nothing. It is merely a pleasant whim of mine. Imagine the touching reunion. The smiling surprise of the mother. Why, it will be as good as a play to watch.'

Bored, Dan reached for the chocolate pot to pour himself a cup of chocolate.

'Francis is right, Father,' said Selina. 'We do it for our own amusement. And think how well Betty will work when she owes us such a debt of gratitude.'

'Betty?' Dan looked up quickly.

His father frowned. 'I had hoped you were too chastened to speak,' he said disapprovingly. 'I looked for penitence. Still, I suppose you may gain improvement from hearing of the good deed your brother and sister plan to do for our little rocker.'

Dan felt the hair prickle on the back of his neck. 'Good deed?' he repeated stupidly.

Selina crumbled her toast. 'The poor wretch is homesick,'

she said in a casual voice. 'Imagine. She pines for her family and the hovel where they live. So Francis and I intend to take her on a visit tomorrow. It will make a pleasant drive.'

'A pleasant drive! Thirty miles in a day for no real purpose.' Sir Horatio shuddered delicately. 'With the start before dawn. Even with a change of horses, it will be a tedious journey.'

'You forget, Father,' Francis said baitingly, 'that we are tougher than you are. We have good merchant blood in us.'

Predictably, Sir Horatio stiffened at this mention of his wife's connections and Francis went on teasing him gently, leaving Dan time to think.

Betty? Homesick? Brisk, down-to-earth Betty pining and languishing? It sounded like nonsense. He tried to catch Selina's eye, but she looked away evasively. Gulping down his cup of chocolate and his piece of toast as quickly as he could, he stood up to leave the table.

'So little breakfast?' Sir Horatio raised an eyebrow.

'I beg your pardon, Father, but I think I should go to my lesson. I must make my peace with Mr Heron.' The lie slid on to his lips, and it seemed to satisfy his father, who dismissed him with a nod. The next moment, Dan was flying up the stairs towards the nursery, to find the only person who might tell him what was going on.

Betty and the nurse were dressing the baby for the day. The nurse held the child on her knees, while Betty pulled on the embroidered dress and the linen cap. Dan said the first thing that came into his head.

'Nurse, my mother would like to speak to you. I think she is in the drawing-room.' That should take time to unravel, for Lady Merrowby was certainly still in bed. As the nurse bustled off down the stairs, Dan whispered, 'What do I hear about a trip to your home? Has it anything to do with what we saw in Exeter?'

When Betty looked up, her eyes were blank. 'I'm sure I don't know what you mean, Master Daniel. And the less said about what we saw at Exeter, the better it will be.'

'What?' He stared at her, bewildered. 'Last time we talked, you thought it all a great joke.'

'I did?' Her face was prim as she tied the baby's cap strings.

'Yes, you did. You've changed. There's something strange about you.'

Betty shrugged, and suddenly a suspicion jumped into Dan's mind. 'I know what it is,' he said fiercely. 'You see nothing wrong in smuggling. So you have joined with them. You're going to help them make another landing.' He looked at her in disgust. 'How much are they paying you?'

'Paying me?' Betty turned bright red. 'Think I'd take money to help 'em? With that? Oh, 'twas fine enough and funny when I thought there was brandy or tea in the coffin. Does no harm to anyone, that. Only the government, and who cares for them? Everyone does that. But 'twas not brandy. Nor tea neither. That coffin was jampacked with Chantilly lace. Ten thousand, maybe fifteen thousand pounds worth.' She was furious now, and panting hard. 'How much money will be left for the poor lacemakers round Honiton when the factors have bought up all that?'

She stopped, breathless, and Dan looked at her with a frown. He was almost sure that her rage was genuine. 'So what does this new journey mean?' he said slowly.

Betty looked down at the baby, straightening its cap. Her voice was quiet now. ''Tes just a kindness Mr Francis and Miss Selina are doing me. I was lonely for my own folk.'

'Rubbish!' Dan snorted. 'You're not the sort to pine, and Francis is never kind. You're not telling me the truth.' But he could make no sense of it, and Betty, sullen and tight-lipped, did not give any help. 'Whatever it is,' he said at last, 'you should remember that I am not the only person to take an interest. There's someone else. Someone who saw it all.'

'That Mr Ellerby?' Betty sniffed. 'There's no harm in him. Been gone these three days.'

'Gone where?'

She shook her head. 'Back to Italy, likely. To Mr George. What's that to me? I be set to visit my mother.' Her hand trembled slightly on the baby's head. 'You'd best be off afore my aunt comes back. 'Twas a wild-goose chase as you sent her on, I guess. Her'll be none too pleased.'

100

Giving up, Dan limped towards the door. 'I must talk to Sal, then, if I want to know anything.'

''Twill do 'ee no good.' Betty shrugged. 'Her'll not listen to 'ee. Can only make trouble with Whispering Zak.'

She was right, Dan thought gloomily as he went down the stairs. There was no point in trying to talk to Selina. He went along the landing and reached the library just as the nurse panted up from below. Slipping inside, he slammed the door behind him and leaned breathlessly against it, his mind in an uproar. Selina, Francis, Betty, Mr Ellerby. They were like pieces in a mosaic that he could not fit together. But his sense of danger had grown stronger and more threatening. Tomorrow, tomorrow, tomorrow.

'Daniel? Are you all right?'

Looking up, he met Mr Heron's mild, troubled gaze. Suddenly, Dan's brain cleared. He knew what he must do.

'Sir, you promised me that if I needed any help you would give it to me.'

Mr Heron inclined his head, agreeing.

'Well,' Dan said steadily, 'I need to disappear again tomorrow. For the whole day. Without anyone noticing.'

The tutor sat down carefully. 'And I am not to be told why?'

'I can't. I'm sorry. Can you trust me?'

Mr Heron rubbed a hand across his brow. 'I'm afraid you will get yourself into trouble.'

'No, truly. I'm trying to stop trouble for someone else.'

Mr Heron looked at him, weighing him up. 'You have always been a sensible boy,' he said slowly. 'And intelligent. The most intelligent pupil I have ever had. I have never yet found any reason to distrust you.' He thought. 'Can you promise me that what you are doing is necessary?'

'I can't think of any other way to go about it.'

There was a long pause. Then the tutor nodded. 'I have long had it in mind,' he said, 'to take you to visit a friend of mine. A learned Greek scholar who is a parish priest some twenty miles away. We shall go tomorrow. If no one sees us leave, no one will know that we do not go together. And I will meet you – let me see – I will meet you in the hermitage at nine

101

o'clock in the evening, so that we can return together. Does that solve your problem?'

'Yes. Thank you, sir. But what will you do?'

'That is my own affair. I shall see to it that I do not betray you.' He picked up the Latin grammar and let it fall open at the title page, tracing with an idle finger the letters written there. *George Merrowby*, they said. George wrote his name in everything. He liked to own things. The firm, large signature sprawled across the page, ending in an assertive black dot. But Mr Heron did not see it. His thoughts were elsewhere. 'And I hope you will see that you do not betray me,' he said softly. 'It has always been my dream to have a pupil like you, who shared my feeling for the poets. But if this were discovered, it would be the end of our work together.'

'I know that you are taking a risk for my sake,' Dan said gently, 'and I am grateful. I could not have asked it if we were not so –'

He stopped, his voice cracking, and Mr Heron smiled. 'Perhaps we should do some Latin now.'

Francis, Selina and Betty were to leave at dawn. There was no secret about the plan. Sir Horatio and Lady Merrowby discussed it, endlessly and boringly, at dinner that evening. They were so taken up with it that Dan's own visit was hardly remarked upon. It seemed a much more prosaic affair.

'Dawn!' Sir Horatio grimaced. 'A vile, chilly hour. You would do best, I think, to take the travelling chariot. If you are really so foolish as to insist upon driving yourself, Francis.'

'And mind you wrap up warmly.' Lady Merrowby was too controlled to say how much she disapproved of the whole idea, but her opinion was plain.

'We shall be as snug as an old lady by the fireside,' Francis teased. 'Dawn has no terrors for us.'

But Dan knew that he could not trust them to wait until dawn. If he was to be sure of seeing them go, he must spend the whole night watching. And he dared not hide in the stables again, in case Betty should guess and look for him. After much thought, he remembered that the little closet which opened off

102

the drawing-room had one tiny window. From this, he would be able to observe the exit from the stable yard.

As soon as the house was quiet that night, he crept downstairs and shut himself in the closet. The air was stuffy and he could see through the window only by kneeling up uncomfortably on a chair. He smiled grimly to himself. At least he did not risk falling asleep in that position.

All the same, he was dozing and swaying when, after many hours, he suddenly heard voices. A sleepy, enquiring murmur and a reassuring drawl in reply. It sounded as though one of the stable boys had woken. For a while, Dan hoped that the interruption might make Francis abandon his plan. But then a shape came slowly through the arch from the stable yard. Even in the darkness, Dan could see that the travelling chariot was harnessed and on its way, and he knew that he had no time to spare. Quickly, he slipped out of his hiding-place and crept through the silent house and out to the stables.

It was still well short of dawn and, in the darkness, his horse snorted as his fingers fumbled with the harness straps. He was not accustomed to doing the job himself, and the animal was sleepy and recalcitrant. By the time Dan had mounted and set off down the drive, there was no sign of the chariot.

For a quarter of an hour, he rode hard without seeing anything. The moon was nearly full, and it lit up a blank, empty road in front of him. He was sickeningly aware that he might never find them at all. If they were not really going to Honiton, they might have set off in an entirely different direction.

But when he was almost ready to turn and ride home he rounded a corner and there, ahead of him, was a dark shape, its lamps lighting the small circle of road around it. Slowing his horse to a walk, he steered it across to the grassy verge at the side of the road and set himself to follow at a safe distance.

As dawn began at last to colour the sky, the chariot pulled up at a lonely inn. Loitering in a clump of trees, Dan saw that they had stopped to change horses. He fingered the money that he had brought in his pocket, knowing that it would be prudent to do the same. But would the ostler wonder at a boy his age, travelling alone? Putting on his grandest air, Dan rode into the inn yard as soon as the chariot pulled away, his heart beating hard.

He need not have worried. The ostler was too sleepy and bad-tempered to take much notice of him. He just pocketed the money with a surly scowl and led Dan's own horse away to the stable to await his return. Scrambling up on to the nag he had been given, Dan felt his withered leg begin to ache. He had already ridden as far as he was accustomed to, and the road seemed to stretch endlessly in front of him. But he kicked the horse into a trot until he could see the chariot again and then followed once more, nodding sleepily.

It was when they reached Axminster that he suddenly became totally, fearfully awake. The chariot swept through without a pause. But as soon as it had passed, a vehicle pulled out from a lane between two cottages. A squat, black gig, remarkable only for its ugly clumsiness. It drew into the centre of the road and began to follow the chariot sedately. Even though he was still some way behind, Dan recognized the gig and the neat, upright figure in the bag-wig who drove it. With a grim face, he slowed his horse a little more and travelled on, third in the procession.

Chapter 11

THE horses slowed to a walking pace and the chariot began to move slowly down a steep hill.

'Lyme,' Selina said softly. Her face was white and her hands clasped tight in her lap. Betty leaned forward to look through the window as the houses of the little town appeared on either side.

They were shabby and ramshackle, some with broken roofs and shattered windows, obviously empty. Chilly mist hung round them and from below came the ceaseless noise of the waves. It was a cold, wretched setting for what they had to do.

And Selina, sitting rigid and silent, seemed equally cold and wretched. She had hardly spoken, all through the journey. Twisting her hands and biting her bottom lip, she had been sunk in her own thoughts. Now, as the chariot edged its way through the narrow streets, she roused herself.

'Pull your travelling cloak close round you,' she said in a dull voice. 'And I shall put on the veil. They must think we come in mourning. We shall change in a room at the inn.' She took a plain gold ring from her pocket and slid it on to the fourth finger of her left hand. 'Remember, you are my maid. And I am Mrs Burrows of Yeovil.'

'Yes, miss,' said Betty. Then, realizing her mistake, 'Yes, ma'am.' But Selina did not smile.

The chariot swung sideways into the yard of the George and Francis, up in front, jumped down to speak to the obsequious innkeeper.

'Mrs Burrows will need to rest awhile,' they heard him say.

'Please show us to our room. And is our man here already? Good. Send him up in a few minutes.'

'Bring the bag, Betty,' Selina said faintly as Francis handed her out. Fear had made her weak enough to seem a most grief-stricken widow and, as she watched Francis supporting her across the yard, Betty felt a quiver of conscience. All the way, she had wondered whether she would have the determination to betray them when the moment came. She climbed out and dragged the travelling bag after her. As she turned to shut the chariot door, a voice spoke suddenly.

'Ah, you are back, my boy. And how was your uncle?'

It was so near that she looked up automatically. Then she realized that the speaker was in fact through the arch, out in the street. A white-haired old man in a green coat. A stranger. She was about to move away when she heard the second voice.

'B-b-bad tempered as ever. And twice as p-pompous.'

She stopped abruptly, quite still. Was she deceiving herself, or did she recognize that voice? Stepping cautiously sideways, she looked further up the street. And there he was. There was no mistaking those pimples. Nor that queer combination of brown wig and red brows. The nephew of the Exeter Customs Officer had come home to Lyme. Feeling slightly faint, Betty leaned against the side of the chariot.

'B-beautiful morning,' she heard the pimply young man say. 'B-b-breakfast first, I think, and then I shall take a walk along the Cobb. Look at the b-boats.'

For a moment, Betty could hardly breathe. If he walked to the Cobb at the right time, he would see the *Rose of Barnstaple*. And a familiar funeral party. If she stayed silent, he would perhaps do her work for her. And Zachary need never know that she had anything to do with it. All she had to do was keep her mouth shut. Dazed, she walked across the yard and began to climb the stairs of the inn.

As she pushed open the door of the room, she was afraid that the sight of Selina's pale face might soften her into speaking. But Selina had changed. When Betty walked in, she was standing by the window, her head flung up, talking to Francis.

106

'No, I have decided,' she was saying steadily. 'I have been a coward. I shall tell Zachary that he must give up this plan.'

Francis shrugged, an odd expression on his face. 'I do not think you will succeed. But try if you wish. I think he is coming now.'

Betty found that she was shaking slightly as the door opened. She was chilled at the thought of seeing Zachary again. Yet when the innkeeper ushered him in he looked mild enough. The picture of an old family retainer, with a bundle under his arm and his hat held humbly in both hands. The innkeeper shot a curious, doubtful glance at him. But then he looked down at the coin Francis gave him, shook his head and went away.

As soon as the door closed, Zachary's manner changed. He stood up straight and flung his bundle down on to the big wooden chest by the window.

'Get those on. Fast as 'ee can,' he said peremptorily. 'Ship's in already and the tide's right. Sooner we get to the Cobb and 'tes done, the safer 'twill be.' He turned towards the door.

'Wait.' Selina stepped after him, her heavy cloak sliding back off her shoulders. 'Have you considered what I said to you last time we met? This landing is madness. It is too soon after the other one, and too close.'

'Likely.' Zachary's face was guarded.

'I'm sure my brother agrees with me,' Selina went on. 'But all he will tell me' – her mouth twitched with distaste – 'is that he must take his orders from you.'

'Ah, 'tes sour medicine for 'ee.' Zachary smiled and nodded slowly.

'But why are you so determined?' said Selina in desperation. 'Don't you care for your own safety? Can't you see it's foolish?'

Zachary's smile disappeared, and his answering whisper was harsh. 'Think you're the only ones to take physic?'

'What do you mean?'

'He means,' Francis broke in, slowly and wearily, 'that we are all acting under orders. Even him.'

'Him!' Betty was so amazed that she interrupted without

thinking. 'He never works for anyone.' She looked up at Zachary. 'Never.'

'Think I'd do it else?' he rasped back at her scornfully. 'Me? A Devon man? A *Honiton* man?'

'But I don't understand.' Selina sat down suddenly on the wooden chest and stared round at them all. 'There's someone else involved? Who is it?'

'Prior, he calls hisself.' Zachary spat. *'Which* he ain't. Tucked away in Cherbourg he be, with a hand on all our throats. Ask him if you want to slide out.'

Selina looked at Francis. 'Is this true? Who is this Mr Prior?'

Francis shrugged and smiled weakly. 'All I know is that Zachary here brought me a letter signed "James Prior". It told me certain things about myself that – that I had thought were not widely known. And offered silence and a sizeable sum of money in return for my help with his plans. How could I refuse such an offer?'

'But why didn't you tell me this? When you first explained the scheme?'

A quick flicker of amusement crossed Francis' face. 'And would you have joined in with such excitement? If you had known I was being blackmailed into it?'

'Of course not!' Selina said hotly. 'I should have told you to stand up to him, to find out who he was and –' Realizing that she had answered her own question, she faltered. 'So he sits safe in France, taking the money, while we risk everything for him? The man must be a monster!'

'A monster we must obey,' Francis said grimly. 'If we are not to land in prison.'

'Prison?' Zachary creaked with hoarse laughter. 'For smuggling in disguise? No, 'twill be the Bridport dagger for that. The rope.' He let his head fall sickeningly sideways.

Selina shuddered. 'There is nothing we can do, then?'

'You can put on the clothes and make ready.' With a servile, sarcastic bow, Zachary went out. Selina shook herself.

'He may be in the same trouble as we are, but he sets my flesh twitching. To take orders from him!'

Francis smiled thinly. 'It was adventure you wanted. This is

108

the truth of it. Did you think it would be like your precious pirate games? You have no choice. You must change to Mrs Burrows of Yeovil as fast as you can.'

He walked out, slamming the door after him, and Betty bent to fumble with the bundle, to hide her expression from Selina. She did not know what to do. If they were all helpless, all in the power of this Mr Prior, was it right to let them get caught? Yet the only way to make Mr Prior suffer was to let him lose his lace and his money. Unhappily, Betty untied the bundle. Perhaps the Customs Officer's nephew would sit long over his breakfast, and miss the whole thing. Perhaps.

'Hurry up, Betty.' Selina came across and shook out the dresses from the bundle. One black silk, and one black cloth. She picked up the silk one.

'Shall I help 'ee, miss?' Betty said.

'What? Do you think I can't dress myself?' said Selina, with a flash of bravado. 'And me a bold, bad smuggler? No, put on your own. We must make the best showing we can, I suppose.'

The two of them were hardly dressed when there was a light tap on the door. Without any pause for an answer, the door swung open.

'Francis?' Selina said quickly.

But it was not Francis. Selina stared.

'Dan?' she whispered. 'It can't be you.'

'It is me,' he said quietly. Swaying with exhaustion, he limped into the room, his weak leg giving way. 'I followed you on horseback.'

'But you can't –' Suddenly vigorous, Selina slammed the door after him and shook his shoulder. 'You foolish, meddlesome boy! Why did you have to come prying? I thought I had been unkind enough to save you from mixing in this. Now we are all in danger. What am I going to do?'

'Leave 'en, miss,' Betty said softly. ' 'Twas a hard ride for a cripple.'

'But why did he have to come at all?'

Dan staggered and rubbed a hand across his face. 'I thought you would listen to me here. And I have to warn you.' His voice was thick with tiredness. 'You have been followed. Watched. He followed you from Axminster.'

'He?' Selina shook his shoulder again. 'Who?'

Betty had gone pale, but all of a sudden she guessed what Dan must mean. Pushing him gently into a chair, she answered for him. ''Twas him, weren't it? That Mr Ellerby?'

'Mr *Ellerby*?' Selina's eyes widened. 'But what has he to do with anything?'

'He knows everything,' Dan said dully. 'He followed you to the British Lion that night. He was on the quay at Exeter, watching you. And now he is here as well.'

'Exeter?' Selina spun round to face Betty. 'You've been talking.'

Betty shook her head. 'He saw it. But 'tes too long to tell. If that Mr Ellerby's here –'

'I think,' Dan said, 'that he must be some sort of government agent. It's the only thing that makes any sense. He must have come to have you arrested this time. Sal, you have to stop it.'

'But that's impossible.' Selina paced distractedly up and down the room. 'Zachary will not listen to me. What can I do?' She stopped suddenly, decided. 'Betty, run downstairs and fetch Francis.'

But the order was unnecessary. At that moment the door was flung open and Francis walked in.

'Are you going to be all day? Zachary is growling like a bear. He is afraid we shall miss the tide and –' He broke off, drawing in his breath sharply and staring at Dan. 'I thought I had scared you off. And you're here? You little –'

His face was white with anger, but Selina flung herself at him. 'He's come to warn us. He thinks he's a government agent come to have us arrested. You must tell Zachary and make him stop.'

'Wait.' Francis looked at her. 'I don't understand. *Who* thinks *who* is a government agent?'

'Mr Ellerby,' Selina said impatiently. 'Dan said he followed us to the British Lion and to Exeter. And now he is here. He must be going to betray us, in spite of all George has done for him.'

'George would be none too sad to see me in trouble,' Francis said absently. 'He has always envied me the estate Aunt Louisa plans to leave to me. Disgrace would make her disinherit me. But – how clever of Ellerby to find a reason for disgrace.' He brooded, tapping a finger against his teeth.

Selina shook him. 'Oh, what does it matter how he found out? *He knows*, Francis. We are all in deadly danger.'

Suddenly, startlingly, Francis smiled. 'Danger?' he said flippantly. 'With Ellerby watching tenderly over us all? You are being hysterical, Sally.'

'And *you* are being foolish.' Dan exploded. 'It's not a joke. Aren't you going to do anything?'

'Ah, our observant little brother.' Francis looked up. 'Always appearing in unexpected places. Jealous because you were left out. Come here.'

'You're wasting time,' Dan said doggedly.

'Come here.'

Standing up, Dan hobbled across the room while Betty and Selina watched Francis in puzzlement. The weary, cynical expression he had worn all day was suddenly gone and, instead, he had an air of controlled excitement, as if something pleased him. As Dan approached, he stood up and caught him by the shoulder.

'Well,' he said softly, 'since you have seen so much, perhaps you should see something more.'

He turned the little brass key which locked the chest he had been using as a seat.

'Look.' He threw up the lid and, obediently, Dan leaned over to peer in.

'But it's nothing,' Betty heard him say, bewildered. She could see that the chest held only a heap of spare blankets.

'Nothing yet.' With whiplash speed, Francis thrust a hand in Dan's back, pushing him face downwards among the blankets. With the other hand, he jerked his legs in after him. Then, sitting down quickly on the lid, he turned the key once more.

'There.' He looked with satisfaction at Betty and Selina. 'One spy at least is taken care of.'

'But you can't leave him there,' Selina protested from across the room. 'He'll suffocate.'

There were only muffled noises coming from the chest. Francis stood up, brushing off his hands.

'If we leave him to wander round the town,' he said coldly, 'we shall all lose our breath for ever. In a much more unpleasant way. He is sure to cause trouble. Don't fuss, Sal. There's room enough in there. He'll be all right.'

Selina looked doubtfully at the chest and then walked to the door. 'You're sure?'

'Of course I'm sure,' Francis said soothingly. 'It won't be for long, Sally. As soon as the landing is safely over, we'll be back to let him out.'

'If we come back.' Selina was pale.

'We'll come back. Everything will be splendid. As long as we don't loiter now. Come on.' Francis was full of a kind of triumphant gaiety as he opened the door.

Betty did not understand it. But she knew one thing, with cold certainty. He was taking a risk with Dan's life. The chest was so full of blankets that there could be very little air inside. And Dan was weak and exhausted from his long ride. Selina would never let him stay there if she had seen. Betty nearly opened her mouth to tell her. Then she had a better idea. As she walked past the chest, she stumbled and fell, dropping her cloak.

'Come on, girl, come on,' Francis said impatiently, looking round. 'No one will take you for a lady's maid if you are as clumsy as that.'

'No sir. Sorry, sir.' She got up quickly, pulled the cloak round her and pattered through the door, leaving Francis to lock it behind them.

He had not heard, she thought, relieved. His ears had not caught the faint click of the brass key beneath the folds of her cloak when she scrambled up. At least Dan would be able to breathe until they got back. If they were lucky enough to get back at all.

112

Chapter 12

*A*s his face thudded down on to the blankets, Dan had been too surprised to resist. But the lid, banging down, caught the back of his head and sobered him. He heard the key turn to lock him in and he tried to think. Breathe. He had to breathe. There was very little room to struggle, but he pressed his hands hard on the blankets under his face and made a small space in which he could gulp a few mouthfuls of stuffy air.

He did not hear Betty unlock the chest again, but he heard the three pairs of feet leave the room and he knew that he had to do something quickly before he was smothered. He would have to try and break the lock. Gathering his strength, he pushed down with his knees and hands and arched his back sharply.

Rather to his surprise, the heavy lid flew open at once and he was so relieved that for a moment he could not move. He just lay trembling and gasping for breath, still cocooned. When he scrambled out, he hurried to try the door. It was locked.

His first instinct was to bang on it, to summon someone from the inn to let him out. But he realized quickly that it would only lead to suspicion and trouble. Walking back across the room, he made himself sit on the chest and think.

He did not believe that Francis had meant to kill him. Throwing him into the chest had been an act of bravado, impetuous thoughtlessness. They were both the same, Francis and Selina. They did things in the heat, without pausing to see the consequences. He knew that he was different. He could not act fast, but, like George, like Grandfather Turner, he could plan ahead and see where things were leading. He forced himself to work things out slowly now, with an eerie feeling that the safety of them all might depend upon it.

The obvious thing was to stay where he was. To make certain of his own safety. That was what George would have done. Then, if the others came back, he could go home with them. If not, he could escape at leisure and still go home.

But that made nonsense of his exhausting ride through the dawn. What had he come for, if not to help Selina? If he wanted to do that, he must get out of the room and follow to watch. And the door was locked. Kneeling up on the chest, he examined the window.

It opened on to a short drop down to a sloping roof. For anyone else, it would have meant a quick jump, a slither down the roof and a drop to the ground. With his withered leg, Dan was hampered and he stared out for a couple of minutes before he unlatched the diamond-paned casement and clambered on to the windowsill. Curiously, there was no one in sight in the inn yard below. Dan had expected to see people bustling about, but the whole place was deserted. Puzzled but relieved, he lowered himself out of the window and dropped the short distance to the tiles, jarring his back as he took the weight on his good leg. He slithered down the roof and looked over his shoulder, down at the cobbled yard. It was further away than he had thought, and for a second he wavered.

Then he seemed to hear Selina's voice in his ear. *Come on Morgan, me old shipmate. Stap me, we'll never take this merchant-man if you can't swarm up her side!* She had never had any mercy on his weak leg and, remembering that, he had no mercy himself. He slipped over the edge of the roof and fell on the cobbles.

Because his legs were uneven, he landed awkwardly, banging his twisted knee on the knobs of stone, so hard that he winced. But he was down and, scrambling to his feet, he found that he could walk, even though it was painful. He bit his lip and limped across the yard towards the arch.

At once, he was surrounded by people. The whole town seemed to be on the move. He was carried along the street towards the seashore and all the time more people spilled out

114

of doorways and ran along the road, calling to each other.

'Annie! Do 'ee come back this instant!' a woman shouted from a wide road to his right. 'Leaving the lace!'

Dan tensed for a moment, and then realized. She was not speaking of the smuggled lace. They were lacemakers themselves. In some of the open doorways, he could see the humps of lace pillows, with their bobbins left idle. The lacemakers ran down the hill, and the girl, Annie, called back up to her mother, 'Oh, Mam, do 'ee come too. Lace'll wait. 'Tes a proper sight. Hearse's driving along to the Cobb. Customs Officer hisself be gone.'

With a shrug, the mother pulled her door to and joined the crowd which hurried along the shore.

Lyme was so small that, normally, a stranger like Dan would have been noticed. But now it seemed that the whole population was taken up with curiosity about the hearse. Everyone pushed along the beach towards the Cobb, whose curved wall made the harbour. Figures scrambled over breakwaters. Ragged, dirty children. Women with babies on their hips. A few rough-looking men. More and more of them darted out from the decaying buildings, as lively as if they were going to a fair. Stepping down on to the sands, Dan limped along with them.

He could see the spiky masts of the ships clustered in the harbour. Somewhere among them was the *Rose of Barnstaple*, no doubt, with its load of contraband. And ahead of him he could see the black shapes of the hearse and the coaches, rolling through the shallow water at the shoreline. Selina would have an audience for her performance this time. Dan prayed that none of the watchers would realize that it was play-acting indeed.

The procession drew up on the beach by the harbour and two figures climbed from the second coach. Francis and a brisk little man who must be the Customs Officer. Dan saw Francis nod gravely. The Customs Officer nodded back accommodatingly and waved a hand. Out in the harbour, far up the Cobb wall, sailors moved on board a ship. Something was lowered over her side.

115

''Tes the coffin, see?' A woman next to Dan prodded her neighbour excitedly. 'Poor soul. Fancy dying in foreign parts, away from your own. They're bringing 'en ashore now.'

With slow dignity, some of the sailors took the coffin on their shoulders and began to pace along the wall. There was no sign of Selina, but Dan could see Zachary on the box of the hearse, his bony face sombre and his grey hair, tied back, ruffled by the steady sea breeze. Beside the hearse, four bearers stood with bowed heads, waiting for the coffin, and in front four horses tossed their heads restively.

The sailors stepped on to the sand and set down the coffin at the feet of Francis and the Customs Officer, who took off their hats reverently. Just at that moment, a man moved in front of Dan, blocking his view, and, tense with anxiety, he tried to wriggle past so that he could see.

The man looked round as he felt himself pushed. There was a brief, appalled pause as the two of them recognized each other. Then Mr Ellerby's hand shot out and gripped Dan's wrist pulling him round to stand in front.

'You will see better from there,' he murmured quietly. 'But don't dare to move. It would be most unseemly to disturb this sad occasion.'

Dan was speechless. He could not escape. He could not even turn round to face Mr Ellerby, for the secretary's fingers gripped his shoulders, digging in cruelly. And there was no way of guessing what he was going to do, because his face had been as bland and unhelpful as ever. All Dan could hope was that he would be ready when Mr Ellerby made his move, so that he could trip him or hold him back in some way. Grimly alert, he fixed his eyes on the funeral party.

'Poor little creature,' murmured an old woman at his elbow. 'Look, her's only young.'

Selina was coming down the steps of the first coach, with the same frail but determined air that she had worn the last time. And, with the same feebleness, she staggered at the foot of the steps and had to be steadied by Francis. The women round Dan were moved and sympathetic.

'Overcome by it all.'

116

'Poor duck. No wonder.'

Dan was moved in a different way. Something about Selina's manner, about the set of her head, told him that she was terrified. At Exeter, she had been enjoying herself, but now she knew the danger, and Dan guessed that her faintness was more real than assumed. Digging his nails into the palms of his hands, he willed her not to pass out.

And it seemed that she would manage it. Indeed, there was even less trouble than there had been at Exeter. The Customs Officer was plainly as touched as everyone else by the sight of the brave and desolate young widow. He bowed to her and blew his nose on a large, white handkerchief. Then he flapped his hand towards the hearse, to indicate that the bearers might take up the coffin. And Mr Ellerby, behind Dan, still had not moved.

But, all of a sudden, there was a stir in the crowd. A tall young man pushed his way through. Dan glanced at him, puzzled. Surely that face was familiar? Yet he could not put a name to it.

'Wait! P-please wait!' The young man's voice came crisply through the cold air and the group of figures at the waterside stopped moving. Everything was still, except where the wind ruffled Selina's veil and the grey streamers of Zachary's hair.

The young man strode across the beach, towards the funeral party, his pimply face red with embarrassment. 'I have watched this very scene b-before,' he called to the Customs Officer. 'Open the coffin.'

Then Dan remembered. His skin turned icy and, from behind, the fingers dug harder into his shoulders.

But before the Customs Officer could answer, Zachary's bowed head snapped suddenly upright. With a flick of the reins, he started the hearse moving towards the road on his right, which led away from the town. The bearers and the two coachmen leaped on to the flat back of the hearse and Francis sprinted after and vaulted on beside them.

'Stop them!' yelled the Customs Officer.

The pimply young man started forwards and the crowd eddied half-heartedly after him, along the beach. But before anyone caught up with the hearse there was a sharp crack. The young man fell to the ground, clutching his shoulder, and everyone else stopped, staring at the smoking pistol waving on the back of the hearse.

'Keep after them!' the Customs Officer bellowed, red in the face. 'You can catch them going up the hill.' He himself was rooted to the spot, his fingers tight round Selina's wrist, but he flapped his other hand urgently at the crowd.

All round him, Dan could hear rebellious mutters.

'Good luck to 'em. I bain't risking a ball in the face.'

'Not for Customs, leastways. Bit of brandy never did any harm.'

'Neat a scheme as I ever heard tell of.'

'If he wants 'em chased, he can chase 'em hisself.'

There was a grudging admiration in the voices, as the crowd stood watching the hearse rattle up the hill and out of sight. The empty coaches stood deserted on the beach, their horses champing fretfully. And in front of them was Selina, her wrist imprisoned in the Customs Officer's hand.

Gradually the crowd pressed closer, across the respectful space that had been left before, eager to see the coffin opened. Dan and Mr Ellerby were pushed with them and Dan saw the Customs Officer, still holding Selina, signal to the sailors to open the coffin. The wooden lid creaked protestingly as it was levered up. One of the sailors lifted it up and dropped it with a thud on the sand.

'My God!' the Customs Officer said.

The young man had struggled to his feet. Now, still clutching the reddening patch on his shoulder, he walked over to the open coffin and bent down, pulling out part of the bundle inside. It hung lightly from his hands, fluttering with exquisite delicacy in the cold breeze.

'Devils!' someone breathed, close to Dan.

''Tes lace!'

Visibly, the mood of the crowd changed. Till then, everyone had been silent, still sympathetic to Selina. Even as a smuggler, she had their admiration. But at the sight of the lace they began to press forwards, shouting abuse.

118

'Taking the bread from honest folks' mouths!'

'Filthy foreign trash!'

The young man straightened and stepped closer to Selina. Awkwardly, he lifted her veil and flung it back over her head. Her face was completely white. Almost sadly, he said, 'I knew I could not have forgotten you.'

But Selina was not looking at him. She was staring at the hostile crowd, her lips parted and her eyes wide. At every threatening shout, she winced.

'Come on then, madam!' The Customs Officer shook her shoulder roughly. 'We have you, at least.'

As if his words had woken her, Selina jerked her head round suddenly, her face fierce. ''Tes a fine thing thee's done!' she yelled. 'But us'll get 'ee yet. Thee can be sure of that!'

Dan blinked. What was she doing? Why was she speaking in that rough Devon accent? To add to his confusion, he heard a soft chuckle from over his shoulder. Mr Ellerby was amused.

But there was no time to think. The Customs Officer shouted, 'Take her to the Cockmoil. She'll be secure there till she's sent to Dorchester.'

He began to drag Selina along the beach towards the town, and one of the men from the crowd joined in, catching her by the shoulders and rushing her almost off her feet. More men picked up the coffin, to carry the lace to the Customs House, and the whole throng of people turned, pressing back towards Lyme. Only Dan glanced back over his shoulder. He saw a small figure, wrapped in a heavy cloak, duck out of the far side of one of the deserted coaches and lose itself in the crowd. He had forgotten that Betty must have been sitting there, unnoticed. Quickly he averted his eyes, in case his gaze should give her away.

He and Mr Ellerby were being swept along by the rush of people and he seized the chance this gave him. Quickly, he wriggled out from under the secretary's hands and hobbled on as fast as he could. Normally, he would have had no chance of outrunning Mr Ellerby. He could not outrun anyone. But the whole crowd was set on pursuing Selina, and the press of people separated the two of them and kept Dan at a safe distance. When they began to straggle off the beach and into the town, Dan looked back. Mr Ellerby had vanished.

Dan stumbled on along the street, his eyes fixed on Selina's struggling, yelling figure.

'Devil take 'ee!' she was bellowing. 'Ride off with 'ee and fling 'ee in hell's pit!'

It was an oath she had once made up for Blackbeard, but she yelled it now in a rougher, harsher voice than any she had ever found for the pirate chief. And the crowd yelled its hatred back at her. For a second, Dan's eyes went blank with tears and, in that second, he felt sharp, determined fingers clutch at his arm.

'Leave me alone!' he muttered desperately. 'It's all your fault.' Whirling round, he was ready to spit in Mr Ellerby's smug, discreet face.

But it was not Mr Ellerby's face. It was Betty's. Grim as his own.

'Hush up!' she hissed in his ear. 'Us'd best see where they be taking her.'

'They said the Cockmoil,' panted Dan.

''Twill likely be the blindhouse. Oh,' Betty prodded at him in her impatience, 'the lock-up. You know. Look at the poor soul!'

Unable to escape from the hands which gripped her, Selina still had enough strength to fling herself sideways and drag the whole group askew. Shrieking all the time, still in the same coarse, Devon voice, she clawed and tore at the rough walls of the buildings they passed, clutching at every corner and every projecting stone.

'Dogs, foul stinking dogs!' Her hands waved and scraped and banged against the stones and at every thrust they became more battered, until they were red and bleeding. Dan felt sick at the sight, so wretched that he could hardly think.

'Open up, Tom!' The foremost people were banging on a low, studded door now, shouting to someone inside. 'Us've brought 'ee a pretty bird for thy cage. Open up.'

A harsh laugh sounded in Dan's ear, and he shuddered as Selina was thrust into the gaol, her lowered head banging on

120

the lintel of the door. With a clang, the door shut, and her yells came from inside, muted and wordless. The crowd yelled back, venomously.

'They'll hang 'ee high! That'll teach 'ee to rob honest folks of a living.'

'Thee's a Devon wench! Should've known better.'

''Twill be the Bridport dagger for 'ee, my maid!'

But there was little pleasure in shouting at a closed door. Gradually, the crowd dispersed. People walked off in little muttering groups, without even a glance at the two children who were sidling into a dark alley.

Dan leaned against a building, shaking and terrified, feeling his stomach lurch. Unable to stop himself, he turned aside and vomited, so violently that his whole body seemed to wrench inside out, as if it were trying to rid itself of the memory of the last half-hour. As he straightened, wiping his mouth, he saw that Betty was still at his side.

'Feel better now, do 'ee?' she said cheerfully. 'You've looked ready to throw up, ever since I first saw 'ee.'

'It's easy for you to be calm,' Dan muttered fiercely. 'You wanted them caught, didn't you? If I hadn't seen what happened, I would think it was all your fault.'

He had spoken sourly, out of his unhappiness, but he was amazed by the effect on Betty. Her smile disappeared and she bit hard on her bottom lip. But all she said was, 'I be here, bain't I? Ready to think on how to get her out of that place?'

'What can we do?' Dan said despairingly. 'Two children?'

'So you'll wring your hands and do nothing?' Betty was impatient. 'And Miss Selina gone to all that trouble to give us time?'

'Give us time?' said Dan stupidly.

'Heaven help us, where's your wits? Did 'ee think her shouted like a Devon village wench for a game? 'Twas to keep 'em from finding as her's Sir Horatio's daughter. Long as they don't know that, us'll have time to free her.'

'But there are still only the two of us.'

'Gapesnatch!' Betty stamped her foot. 'Forgotten Whispering Zak, have 'ee? I know where he be. 'Twas all settled afore, in case things went amiss. Password and all. I dare go after 'en if you dare. Us've but to get to Uplyme and –'

She broke off abruptly and laid a warning hand on Dan's arm, gesturing backwards with her head. A small, grubby boy was standing at the corner of the street, watching them with interest. Dan's mouth dropped idiotically open as he realized what an odd picture they must present. His clothes marked him out clearly as richer, better-born than Betty. And yet she had been standing over him with an air of command. Questions, even from a little boy, could bring all sorts of trouble.

But Betty had thought more quickly. 'I minds 'en, see?' she said pleasantly to the boy. 'He's – you know.' And she tapped her head and winked.

The boy's eyes travelled from Dan's clumsy boot to his open-mouthed face and back again.

'He be dangerous?' he said, awed.

Betty shrugged. 'None so bad. Leastways, when he don't bite.'

That settled the little boy. He ran off, glancing nervously over his shoulder. Betty looked apologetically at Dan.

''Twas the best way. To get rid of 'en quickly.'

'It was ingenious,' said Dan with a bitter grimace. 'And no wonder he took me for an idiot. I was standing here as empty-headed. You were right. There is no use lamenting. We must do something. I should still have a horse in the stables at the Three Cups. We'll go to Uplyme. And Whispering Zak.'

They were so impatient that the journey seemed endless. But at last they reached a tumbledown cottage, just short of Uplyme. Betty scrambled from behind Dan on the saddle and tapped lightly, three times, on the door.

''Tes shut,' growled a voice from inside. 'There be no beer here today.'

Carefully, Betty said, 'Think I want thy rotten beer? Every-one knows 'tes stinking swill.'

Slowly the door opened a little and a dark, bearded face looked doubtfully through the crack.

'Children!' It was a surly mutter. 'Be off!'

122

'Be off thesself,' Betty said briskly. 'Ax those as be in there if Mrs Burrows didn't bring a little maid along.'

The door slammed in her face, but she went on standing stubbornly there and after a few moments the door was opened again.

'Get in, then,' said the voice reluctantly. 'Hope there's none to see 'ee.'

Betty and Dan slid through the door and the alehouse keeper stared sullenly at them. Then he gestured towards a hole in the floor. 'They be down in the cellar. Quick now. I'll have to shut the trap door after.'

The hole gaped downwards and, as Dan dangled his legs into it, Betty shuddered. ''Tes like the mouth of Hell.'

It was her only sign of fear. Without wavering, she climbed on to the ladder behind Dan and began to reach for the next rung with her foot. As Dan reached the ground, he turned to look at the scene in the damp, shadowy cellar.

On the earth floor, Zachary's men were huddled, squatting in a group that formed a single, solid shape in the flickering light of the candle on the table. At the table, sitting on stools, were Francis and Whispering Zak.

And between them, his face as unmoved and expressionless as ever, his hands clasped lightly on the table top in front of him, was the neat, self-contained figure of Mr Ellerby.

Chapter 13

DAN stopped dead, pinning Betty on the ladder.

'Get on then!' She shoved impatiently at him and he stepped aside without speaking, so that she was taken by surprise when she turned. That sneaking little Mr Ellerby. Sitting there as calm as you please. Her breath hissed.

'Well, well,' said Francis, 'here you are *again*, little brother. You are certainly persistent.'

'What is *he* doing here?' Dan pointed at Mr Ellerby.

'Ah yes,' Francis answered quickly, not giving Dan a chance to say any more. 'Your spying government agent. I'm afraid you were mistaken about that, Dan. This gentleman has a perfect right to be here.'

'An amusing mistake.' Mr Ellerby did not look in the least amused. He was watching Dan closely. 'My interest in this affair is of quite a different kind. I was sent to observe events by – by the gentleman who put up the money for the venture.'

Betty saw Dan frown, but it was impossible to tell what he was thinking. And before he could speak, Francis broke in.

'You did not know that all of us here were acting under orders from France? Ah, perhaps I have overestimated you. We are working for a gentleman by the name of Prior. Of Cherbourg.'

Dan looked silently from Francis to Mr Ellerby. And back again. It was Zachary who broke the hush.

'Mr Prior, the master,' he croaked sourly. 'Him as holds us all in the palm of his hand.' He cupped his long fingers on the table, like claws, and Betty felt Dan seize her own hand and squeeze it savagely.

'Mr Prior?' he said, in a hesitant voice.

Zachary spat.

'I would remind you all,' said Mr Ellerby smoothly, 'whatever you may feel about Mr Prior, that he has put you in the way of making a good deal of money. It is unfortunate that things have gone awry, but we owe it to him to work out a plan for recovering his lost cargo. I'm sure you see the sense in that.'

Zachary snorted. 'You mean he'll bring us all to the gallows else.'

'But I don't understand.' Dan dropped Betty's hand and went red in the face. 'The lace? What does that matter? We must get my sister out of prison.' He took a step forward and spoke directly to Mr Ellerby. 'Don't you think that Mr Prior would say that was the most important thing?'

Mr Ellerby's eyes shifted, almost as if he were embarrassed. 'I think,' he said levelly, 'that Mr Prior has a lot of money invested in the lace. He would not wish to lose it.'

'Don't be a child, Dan,' Francis broke in bitterly. 'You're like Sal, with a head full of death or glory. This is real life, and in real life it is Mr Prior's money that matters.'

Betty felt Dan shake. Looking sideways at him, she saw that his face was pale. He was staring at Francis in a stunned, bewildered way. Betty felt a sudden spurt of rage. She stepped forward and banged a fist on the table, thrusting her face at Zachary.

'And you'll let her hang? Round Honiton way, they say as you never let your own be taken. 'Tes the only good I ever heard of 'ee.'

Zachary shrugged. 'Her's none of mine. Rich folks can shift for theirselves.'

'You'd rather take the lace?' Betty pulled a scornful face. 'Spite your own folks as make good Honiton stuff? I thought you were a Devon man. Sold your conscience to this Mr Prior, have 'ee?'

'Think I'd do it for choice?' Wearily, Zachary looked down at

125

his hand, still cupped on the table. 'I told 'ee. He has us all like this. And I can't even find out who he is.' His whisper sank to an evil murmur. 'But I tell 'ee, if I could find his real name, why, the lace could go hang. I'd have 'en!' The bony fingers suddenly clamped viciously shut, so hard that the knuckles whitened. Zachary's eyes kindled.

Dan took a quick step forwards, but Francis was still watching him.

'Sit down, Dan. You've meddled enough. Now be quiet. We have no choice but to make a plan to recapture the lace.'

Staring at Francis, Dan slumped down into a corner away from Zachary's men, and Betty sat down beside him. Poor soul. Hard as a horse he was breathing, and his whole body trembling. She patted his arm soothingly and murmured, 'There's nothing can mend things.'

'But there is!' Dan muttered urgently. 'It's there, as clear as day. Why doesn't Francis –'

He had been talking almost to himself and now he stopped, frowning and rubbing his head fiercely. Betty did not understand what he meant, but, looking at Francis, she knew why he had done nothing. His hands, clutching each other behind the back of his chair, were shaking visibly. Mr Prior had him by the throat, and he was scared out of his wits.

The three at the table had their heads together, whispering plans, while Zachary's men stirred and mumbled on the other side of the cellar. Zachary was talking steadily, but it was Mr Ellerby who nodded approval or disapproval.

'It's as clear as day,' Dan said again, so softly that Betty could hardly hear him. He looked almost ready to faint. 'And Francis was right about one thing. This is real life, not a game. If he won't do it, I will.'

Taking even Betty by surprise, he jumped to his feet and interrupted the whispers at the table in a loud voice.

'Francis! Won't you persuade Zachary to help save Sal? You know you can.'

'Sit down!' Francis's hands clenched tighter behind his chair.

But Zachary had turned to look at Dan. 'Let the lad speak.'

126

'What would you do, Zachary,' Dan's chest heaved as he took a deep breath, 'if you knew Mr Prior's real name? Would you inform against him?'

Zachary laughed shortly. 'And have 'en tell all he knows about us? I bain't such a tomnoddy. If I knew, I could find 'en and deal with 'en. In private.'

Dan gulped again. 'Well, I can tell you who he is. If you really want to know.'

'Thee?' Zachary gave a disbelieving snort, but his eyes were grave, taking in Dan's desperate earnestness. Betty saw that Francis and Mr Ellerby had become utterly still. Zachary did not miss it either. He made a quick movement with his hand and two of his men stood up and moved threateningly behind the chairs. A slow suspicion began to grow, incredibly, in Betty's mind.

'I know who Mr Prior is,' Dan said, looking as if he were about to be sick again. 'And I'll tell you. When you have got my sister free.'

Zachary's eyes narrowed. He looked at Francis and Mr Ellerby. Then back at Dan. 'Think I be such a fool?' he said warily. 'When her's free, thee'll say 'twas all a joke.'

Dan stared steadily back at him. 'You don't believe that. You can see that Francis and Mr Ellerby know what I'm thinking, and they haven't said I'm wrong. *Because I'm right.*'

Glancing meaningfully at his men, Zachary slowly drew out his knife, turning it so that the blade flashed suddenly in the candle-light. Two of the gang caught at Dan's arms and dragged him round in front of the table, within striking distance of the sharp steel edge which lay, wickedly still, on the table.

'I be a proper impatient man,' Zachary said mildly. 'Perhaps thee'd do best to tell me now. If thee knows.'

Dan breathed hard, but he did not waver, although one of the men twisted his arm cruelly behind his back. 'You've heard my bargain. Not until my sister's free. If you kill me now, you'll never know.'

Zachary frowned, and then a smile spread slowly over his face. 'Thought thy family was all milk and water,' he whispered, 'but thee's as true steel as my knife. Thee and thy sister both. 'Tes only that one –' he jerked a contemptuous thumb at Francis – 'as'd trade anything for his neck. Leave the lad be.'

The heavy hands dropped from Dan's arms and he shook himself slightly. Without glancing away, Zachary called over his shoulder to the rest of his men. 'You've heard the lad. What'll it be? The wench, or Mr Prior's lace?'

The men moved in the shadows.

'Her's a proper brave maid.'

'Haven't sent the officers to take us.'

Dan was holding his breath. One after another, the men stood up, their heads stooped under the low ceiling.

'That Prior, he don't care nothing for us.'

'A child could've told 'en 'twas too soon for another landing.'

They pressed towards Zachary, a solid wall of flesh and bone, and he nodded. 'Us'll free her then? And after,' he ran a finger evilly along the blade of his knife, 'us'll settle scores with *Mr Prior*.'

The men began to laugh, suppressed, choking laughter that echoed suffocatingly in the close, crowded cellar. Zachary stilled them with a raised finger.

'No time for that. Us've got to make a plan. Seven men and two children, us be. 'Tes too few to take the place.'

'Eight men,' said Francis suddenly. 'Do you think I should not prefer to rescue my sister, given the chance?'

'Nine men.' Mr Ellerby leaned across the table and smiled, thin-lipped, at their surprise. 'I spoke before for Mr Prior, as was my duty. But now I speak for myself. I am happy to help a young lady as brave as Selina Merrowby. And perhaps I may be of use to you. My face was not seen among the funeral party.'

Studying their faces, Zachary nodded. But he did not move his men from behind their chairs. Instead, he beckoned the two children closer. ''Tes a hard plan to make,' he rasped. 'To take her from the very middle of the town. A shout from the gaoler will fetch a hundred men.'

'Couldn't we lure the gaoler out?' Dan said diffidently. 'We could send a message saying there is a plot to recapture the lace. It's nearly the truth, after all.'

'Aye,' said Zachary sourly, 'and who are we to send as a messenger? Think he won't guess as 'tes one of us?'

'There's one messenger as we can send,' Betty said slowly. 'A messenger as be no messenger. Dan, do 'ee remember how I made 'ee out to be an idiot?'

'Him? There's no one as'd take *him* for an idiot,' muttered Zachary scornfully. 'Sharp as a sack of monkeys, that one.'

'No, *listen*.' Betty began to talk quickly and Dan, catching her idea, let his mouth hang open and his head roll sideways, as if it were too heavy for his neck. The men chuckled appreciatively and a look of interest grew on Zachary's face. Taking over, he started to give orders, to turn Betty's idea into an organized plot. Dan leaned forward in excitement, completely absorbed, but Betty found that she was distracted in an odd way.

All the time Zachary was talking, she was aware of Mr Ellerby's cold eyes resting calculatingly on Dan's face.

Chapter 14

*T*HOMAS Wade was bored. He had not expected to be bored. When they brought the girl into the Cockmoil, she had been struggling hard and screaming in a rough Devon voice, and his tongue had moved with relish over his thick, clumsy lips. There would be fine amusement in tormenting her when the Customs Officer had done with his questions.

But as soon as the questions started, she had become like a statue, cold and rigid. For over an hour, the Customs Officer and his men had tried to bully from her the names of the rest of the gang, but she looked back defiantly at them, her head held high, saying nothing. And when at last dinner time came and the men went away, the Customs Officer looked hard at Thomas. 'Have a good eye to her. And none of your tricks, mind. I don't want to see a mark on her.'

So there she was, slumped in gloom on the sandy floor, staring down at her knees. There was nothing else to look at in the dark-house. No table, no chairs, nothing that could possibly be used as a weapon. Thomas watched her sulkily as he paced up and down the little cell. Three steps from one side to the other. Five steps from end to end. As he passed her, he aimed a kick that did not quite touch and muttered, 'There's plenty as hates thee out there. Nothing worse than a lace smuggler.'

She tossed her head at that, her lip trembling. He tried again. 'Proper fine young lady was 'ee, out there? Bin found out now, hasn't 'ee?' But this time she did not move, did not even look up, and, disgusted, he resumed his pacing.

He was so bored that he was easily distracted by the children's voices squabbling outside. The first one was thick and stumbling, an idiot's voice.

'Take that! And that! And that! I'll bang you and thump you and shoot you!'

Then a girl's voice, quieter and urgent. 'Hush now, Master Frederick. Be quiet, or someone'll hear 'ee.'

'*They* won't hear me,' the idiot's voice babbled. 'Up to the Customs House they're going. With pistols and sticks, pistols and sticks, pistols and sticks. Bang! Bang! Bang! I'll die you dead and have my lace back.'

'Ssh, now!' There was an edge of terror to the girl's voice, and then the sound of a sharp slap. 'They'll kill 'ee if they hear. Should never have listened to 'em.'

Slowly, through the sound of the idiot's whimpers, the words penetrated Thomas's dull brain. He glanced quickly at his prisoner. She had looked up when the squabbling began, but now her head had sunk back on to her chest and she was deep in her own thoughts. Crossing to the window, Thomas reached up and peered through the little iron grating. He could see the two outside now. The idiot, his left foot dragging in its heavy boot, was stumbling up and down, muttering rebelliously. 'Pistols and sticks! Pistols and sticks!' The girl – a maidservant, from her dress – was hauling desperately at his arm. 'Hush up, now!'

'Here, wench!' shouted Thomas. 'Come over here.'

Startled, the girl looked round and then, reluctantly, came across to the window. Thomas gestured at the idiot.

'What do he say?'

'Honest, sir, 'tes nothing.' The girl was gabbling, clearly frightened. 'He's simple. You can see. Don't do to take no account of what he says.'

'Pistols and sticks! Pistols and sticks!' Beaming foolishly, the idiot pranced up to the window and pointed a finger at Thomas. 'Bang! I've killed you. Like the big man said he would.'

'Big man? What big man?' Thomas glanced quickly over his shoulder to make sure his prisoner had not moved. Then he pulled a coin out of his pocket. 'Here, I'll give 'ee this if thee tells me.'

'Be quiet now, Master Frederick,' said the maid sternly.

'I want. I want the penny. And I did see the big man. He was angry, because they took away his lace.'

'And what will he do?' wheedled Thomas, wishing he could give the boy a good shaking.

'Give me the penny, and I'll tell you.'

Thomas tossed the coin through the window. The idiot grovelled in the dirt for it, bit it and stowed it in his pocket. Then he beamed. 'The big man's going to kill them all. While they're not there. While they're having their dinner. He's going to bring his men, with pistols and sticks, pistols and sticks, pistols and sticks.'

Chanting, he capered off and the little maid frowned up at Thomas. ''Tes nothing, sir. Just something as he heard. And I be set to mind 'en. 'Twill be terrible trouble for me if they hear –'

But Thomas was not listening. His mind was full of an idea, and it could hold only one idea at a time. If he sent to tell the Customs Officer that an attack was planned, and he saved the lace, he might do himself a bit of good. Perhaps he might even rise above the boring job of minding prisoners in the Cock-moil.

'Here, wench.' He beckoned her. 'There's a coin for thee too, if thee'll take a message for me.'

'No, sir!' Her eyes big, she backed away. ''Twill be trouble. 'Twill cost me my place if they find he've been awandering again. I can't.'

'But 'tes important!' Thomas shouted.

It was too late. The girl had run over to the idiot and caught at his arm. She dragged him past the Guildhall and away. Even as Thomas shouted, 'Come back!' the two of them vanished round a corner. Desperately, he peered up and down the road, but there was no one in sight. It was dinner time.

For a moment he walked up and down uncertainly. He had been told not to leave his post. All the same, he knew the magistrate. If he failed to pass on this piece of information, and it was discovered –. The prisoner was quiet enough. He could lock her in and be back in five minutes.

Suddenly he decided. Muttering, 'Don't 'ee dare move!' he let himself out of the low door and locked it after him. The street was empty, except for a little group of men, not five steps away. As he moved towards them, the men moved apart to let him pass, some to one side and some to the other. Hurrying between them, with self-important haste, Thomas suddenly found himself facing an old man with lank, grey hair, who smiled politely at him.

'Out of my way, granfer,' said Thomas rudely.

The old man nodded, as if he were about to step aside, and at that moment a blow exploded on to the back of Thomas's head. As he sank to his knees, the world blanking out, he heard the old man whisper, 'Did thy mother never tell 'ee not to speak to strangers?'

Anyone watching would have seen nothing odd after that sudden blow. Just a group of men walking into a dark alley, supporting one of their number who seemed to have drunk too much. Even if there had been anyone to recognise Thomas, there would still have been no surprise. He often drank too much. And in the alley, there was no one to see the rummaging in his pocket, or hear the quick jangle as the keys were pulled out.

Some minutes later, a travelling chariot drew up outside the Cockmoil and a neat, black-coated figure climbed out, with a travelling cloak over his arm.

Betty and Dan, inside, held their breath. Dan had insisted that they should be there, but they could not see anything. The chariot properly held only two, so that they had to crouch on the floor. But they heard the grating sound as the key slid into the lock. Then an old man's voice, completely strange, said, 'What're 'ee at? Opening the dark-house door?'

Dan clutched at Betty's hand, but Mr Ellerby, outside, did not waver. 'Magistrate's orders,' they heard him say smoothly. 'She's to go to the gaol in Dorchester. She'll have to be tried at the Assizes.'

'Ah,' the old man muttered. 'Give 'ee a hand, will I?'

'I think,' Mr Ellerby said coldly, 'that I can manage quite well. Here, you! Girl! Out you come.'

There was the sound of a horrified gasp. 'You!' That was Selina. And a chuckle of relish from the old man. Then the chariot door opened and, in a tumble of petticoats, Selina was pushed in. Mr Ellerby followed, arranging his travelling cloak carefully across his knees as he sat down beside her. Selina was pale and distraught and as she saw Dan and Betty her eyes widened.

'Both of you? We are all taken?'

She burst into tears and, as the chariot pulled away, the old man's voice came floating through the window.

'Come to see 'ee hang, I will! Far as Dorchester, even!'

Dan leaned forward and patted Selina's hand. 'Don't cry, Sal. You're free. It's Francis driving.'

'And no one discovered who you are?' Mr Ellerby asked quickly.

'I saw to that.' Selina wiped her eyes. Then she looked wryly down at her grazed, bleeding hands. 'I made certain that even these would not give me away.'

Betty reached out and touched them timidly. 'They hurt?'

'I'm glad they hurt!' Selina's face was fierce. 'All those people. All that hatred. I never realized we were harming them, and when I heard them – oh, I could have battered my head!' Her voice cracked and she looked round at them all, puzzled. 'But I don't understand. Mr Ellerby?'

'We were wrong about him,' Dan said tightly. 'He works for Mr Prior.'

'Mr Prior?' Selina was confused. Then, suddenly, she gasped. '*Him!* Mr Prior! The man who makes so much money while others risk their necks. I should have guessed it was him. I should have known he never was in Genoa.'

Dan nodded.

'Poor George,' Selina said softly. 'So he has lost his lace. All that money. He will not be well pleased.'

'He has lost more than his lace,' Dan muttered in a stiff voice. 'I had to trade him for you.'

'What do you mean?'

134

''Twas the only way to persuade Zachary,' Betty broke in defensively. 'To promise to tell 'en, when you were free.'

Mr Ellerby licked his lips. 'You're set on keeping your promise, are you, Daniel?'

'Can you imagine trying to cheat Zachary?' Dan pulled a face.

'Oh dear. Oh dear me.' Mr Ellerby shifted slightly in his seat. 'It's all going to be very unpleasant then, isn't it?'

'Unpleasant?' Dan looked up sharply.

'When you tell him,' again the pointed tongue flicked over the thin lips, 'that you don't know who Mr Prior is after all.'

'Why should I do that?' Dan said slowly.

'I think you will see,' Mr Ellerby said evenly, 'that it is the most sensible thing.'

They barely saw him move, but Selina twitched as his hands, under cover of the heavy cloak, thrust sideways at her. Then his left hand flicked away the folds of the cloak so that they could all see what he was holding.

In the shadowy interior of the coach, the pistol barrel gleamed dully, pointing straight at Selina's heart.

It was a neat little pistol, hardly more than six inches long, with elegant arabesques of silver let into the wooden butt. A deadly toy. And in Mr Ellerby's grip it pointed unerringly.

Betty was the first to regain her voice. 'Don't be foolish,' she said quietly. 'What good will it do 'ee to shoot Miss Selina? There's nothing for 'ee but the gallows then.'

Mr Ellerby gave a twisted smile. 'And do you think I can expect a better fate if George Merrowby discovers he is betrayed? Why should you imagine that you are the only ones in his power?'

Dan gulped. 'But if you shoot her, Zachary will still know about George.'

'And she will still be dead,' Mr Ellerby said gravely. 'But I don't intend that either of those things should happen.'

Dan kept his eyes on the pistol, his face frozen. 'What do you want me to do?'

'That is up to you, my dear boy. I suppose you could try to fob Zachary off with another name. But I don't imagine that he will be easily deceived.'

135

'Even when we played pirates,' Selina broke in suddenly, choking, 'we didn't cheat each other, Dan. A bargain is a bargain. Even with Zachary. Even when it's George.'

'But Sal –'

'Don't you think there has been enough deception?' she said wearily.

'You have until you are home,' murmured Mr Ellerby, 'until Zachary catches us up on the borders of the park. When you have had a few hours to think things over, I am sure you will see the sense in my arguments.'

He said no more. No one spoke. It was a long, tense silence. For hours, Dan stared at the pretty little pistol, trying to make a plan, wishing his brain would work faster. But there seemed no way out. Every time the chariot rumbled over a bump or down a pot-hole, he held his breath, in case the finger on the trigger should jerk by accident. And all the time, the country outside grew more and more familiar.

At last Betty said softly. 'Coach is slowing down.'

Behind them, they could hear the sound of hooves coming up. Horses ridden hard. In a few moments, Zachary and his men would be there. The chariot drew to a stop by the back edge of Linhay Park, and Dan swallowed, his throat dry. Mr Ellerby smiled calmly.

'No mistakes, now.' He flicked a fold of his cloak over the pistol, so that it was hidden. A second later, there was a sound of voices outside. Feet jumping down.

Zachary's gaunt face peered through the window and his eyes fastened greedily on Dan.

'My part of the bargain's done, lad. Her's safe home.'

Dan opened his mouth, but no sound came. It was only a tiny hesitation, but at once Zachary's face tightened. With a quick movement, he wrenched the door open and hauled at Dan's coat. He was amazingly strong. Dan found himself dragged out, standing on the road and looking into those chilly eyes.

'Wouldn't be planning to cheat me now, would 'ee?'

'I –' Hopelessly, Dan glanced towards the three in the coach, at Mr Ellerby who was watching him closely waiting for

136

a false move, and at the threatening hump under the cloak. The only thing he could think of was to play for time. Licking his lips, he said, 'Mr Prior is Lord —'

But his eyes flickered and Zachary's hand smashed him across the face. 'Think I'm an idiot?' He spun Dan round, one arm clamped tightly across his chest, and Dan felt the sharp edge of the dagger pressed against his throat.

'I like 'ee, lad,' the harsh voice whispered softly. 'Proper sorry I'd be if — if thee broke thy word.'

Dan could still see into the chariot, where Selina's face was pale in the darkness. There was only one thing he could say.

'I — I can't tell you after all.'

Then he closed his eyes, waiting to feel the blade slice into his throat.

But before Zachary could move, there was a flurry in the chariot. Selina had leaped to her feet, yelling.

'George Merrowby! It's my brother George!'

Her shout was loud enough to carry all along the lane, as if she had crammed into it all the energy of her exhausted body. And her eyes burned with a feverish intensity in her white face. She was tense with urgency, with the need to convince Zachary before his knife hand made its fatal move.

The next instant, there was a sharp crack. Taken by surprise, Mr Ellerby had faltered briefly and then jerked the pistol upwards and fired automatically. Selina screamed and slumped sideways on to the seat, her hands clutched to her face.

Immediately, Zachary dropped his knife and snaked an arm into the coach, pulling Mr Ellerby out. 'Damn 'ee! I had thee wrong.'

Scrambling past them, Dan leaped into the chariot. 'Sal! Sal!'

Almost lazily, she murmured, 'Why, damn you, if I did not now and then kill one of you, you would forget who I am.' Then she fainted and, as her hands fell, Dan saw that her face was covered with blood.

He did not know what to do. He stared at the red drops trickling down and, out of the corner of his eye, he could see

Betty's stunned face, but he could not move.

Then a hand fell on his shoulder. 'Her's not done yet,' whispered a rough voice. 'Take more'n that to kill her.' Zachary leaned over Dan and looked oddly down at Sal. 'Mebbe her'll wish it had, afore her's done,' he muttered. 'Life do lie powerful heavy on some.'

He stopped, as if something choked him, and the next moment he was as sharp and hard as ever, turning to rasp at Francis.

'Get thesself over here!'

Francis was standing slightly back, his face blank and stupid with shock. Glancing at him, Dan was momentarily appalled to see his expression of almost idiotic weakness. But Zachary was too brisk to have any mercy. He moved back and shook Francis hard.

'Get her to that hermitage of yourn. And quick about it. Her needs a woman to tend on her.'

'I'll go ahead,' Dan said quickly, jumping out of the chariot. Now that something could be done, he felt he could speed like a hurricane. 'I'll light the fire and find some candles.'

There was a huddle of men on the road. Zachary's folk were dealing with Mr Ellerby. But Dan did not even spare them a glance. The important thing was to get Sal comfortable. He ran through the little gate into the park and along the winding path which led through the wood to the hermitage.

It was almost dark now, and the gnarled bulk of the hermitage was crouched, like some giant animal, on the far side of the clearing. Dan raced round to the front of it and pushed open the heavy, studded door.

'At last,' said a mild voice. 'I was beginning to wonder what had happened to you.'

He had completely forgotten Mr Heron. Now, watching the tutor set down the glass he had been sipping, he made an instant decision.

'Selina has been shot. Francis is bringing her here. Please help us.'

For a second, as he looked at Dan's distraught expression, Mr Heron's face was full of all the things he could have said.

138

Then he went briskly across to the fire. 'I'll build this up. You light more candles.'

The wood crackled smokily in the hearth and the candle flames leaped high as Betty pushed the door open to let Francis through, with Selina in his arms. Mr Heron took one look and said, 'I'll fetch the nurse.'

'Oh, but –' Betty went pink. 'Aunt Annie's maybe not –'

'She'll come,' Mr Heron said quietly. 'I have a great respect for your aunt. She'll cope with this, however she is.'

As he hurried out, Francis laid Selina gently on the stone bench and covered her with a cloak. Betty looked quickly around.

'Us'd do best to clean that wound. What's that?' She picked up the glass Mr Heron had set down and tasted it, pulling a face. 'Brandy,' she said. 'Good.'

There was a great rip as she tore a panel from her petticoat and dipped one end into the glass. Very gently, she began to wipe the blood from Selina's unconscious face.

'Betty,' Dan said softly, 'that's your petticoat with the lace. That your grandmother made.'

''Tes the finest lawn,' Betty said fiercely. 'My grammer was a great old lady. Her'd never've let Miss Selina go untended. Not for a coffin full of lace.'

She had cleaned all but the wound itself, so that Selina's face was pale, with a clotted red patch on her left cheek, below the eye, when the nurse bustled in with Mr Heron. The old woman's face was drawn and tired, but she took only a single glance before she began to give orders.

'That's right, Betty. There's a good wench. Dan, fetch some clean water. And as for 'ee' – she looked harshly at Francis, who still stood helpless with horror – 'thee'd best get up to the house and tell thy father all. He'll know how to shift. I'll look after Sally.'

The sunlight lay in a small patch on the smooth marble floor of the entrance hall. In the centre of the patch stood Betty, red-faced and stubborn.

139

'You *must* come out,' Dan said firmly. 'They're nearly ready to go.' Over her shoulder, he could see through the open door and into the forecourt, where people scurried round the coach and horses pawed the gravel.

Betty twisted her hands miserably together. 'I can't. I told 'ee, 'twas all my fault. If I'd warned 'em about that man – him with the red eyebrows – they might've stopped away from the Cobb. And none of this would've happened.'

'But you said you didn't want it to happen. Not once you knew about George.'

'You don't understand,' muttered Betty. 'When he spoke, down there on the beach, 'twas as if I'd done it meself, all unwilling. As if I'd put Miss Selina in gaol and then shot her. And do I go out now, all friendly, to say goodbye? And keep my job? With the new nurse? 'Tes wrong, Dan.'

Dan looked at her wearily. 'There's no telling the rights and wrongs of it all. Were we wrong to tell Zachary about George? Or were you and I wrong not to inform on the whole plan to the magistrates? I can't decide. We both kept doing what we *thought* was right.'

'And 'tes right, now, for me to stay?'

'*Please* stay. I want you to.' He held out his hand and, solemnly, Betty took it. For a moment the two of them stood quite still in the middle of the chilly floor, with the pale statues and the dark portraits looking benignly down at them. Then Dan pulled Betty out through the front door to stand at the top of the steps. Below, among the people making polite farewells, the old nurse bustled importantly in her new bonnet and travelling cloak, giving orders to the men who were loading the luggage on to the coach.

'Look,' Dan murmured, 'some things are better than they were before.'

Betty grinned. 'Aunt Annie's always had a fancy to travel abroad. Her's merry as a kitten with it. Planning to keep Mr Francis and Miss Selina in order. And 'twill be best for her. Her's a sight too old for babbies, and her always loved Miss Selina best.'

Suddenly cheerful, she skipped away down the steps to hug

140

her aunt goodbye. Dan limped after, more slowly. He had lifted the cloud from Betty, but it seemed to lie all the more darkly over his own head.

Yet the scene in front of him was gay and elegant. The whole household had gathered to say farewell to Francis and Selina and, in the middle of the crowd, Francis held court, telling some exaggerated tale, his white hand arched expressively to point the joke. Even Sir Horatio, with Lady Merrowby on his languid, silken arm, was smiling appreciatively.

Dan frowned.

'Crosspatch!' said a teasing voice at his elbow. Selina had walked across to him with the caution of someone weak from illness, but the skirts of her travelling dress still swirled and her eye was mocking. Dan could see no more than her eye. The rest of her face was covered by a black silk mask such as her mother, when a girl, had worn to shield her complexion from the sun. 'Does Francis's story not amuse you?'

Dan was nettled. 'How can he be so frivolous? As if nothing had happened?'

The eye behind the black silk mask became suddenly grave. 'So you are deceived by that shell? You too? Do you really think Francis is the same?'

'Just look at him,' Dan said impatiently. Francis with foppish courtliness was handing the nurse into the coach.

'I know,' Selina murmured. 'But he is wounded, Dan, even though you cannot see it. Do you think he will forget how we two acted, while he stood stupidly by? I am not certain that he will ever heal. But I shall try my best to cure him. And I shall have years and years abroad to do it.'

She looked hastily away, as if there were something indecent about watching Francis, and turned towards Dan. 'And now I must go with him and say goodbye to you. I shall miss you, Dan.'

Dan could not begin to say what he felt. Instead, he smiled awkwardly. 'If that were your worst trouble, you would do well.'

'You mean this?' Selina lifted her hand to raise the black silk mask and Dan made a quick movement, as if to stop her.

'Don't. I don't want –'

'Oh, Dan.' Her mouth twisted oddly as she took off the mask, and her good eye blinked hard. Over the other eye, the lid drooped, motionless, and from the corner of it, jaggedly, ran a long, ugly scar, puckered and half healed. Selina flicked at it with her finger. 'You want to remember a beautiful, ladylike sister? At least I have escaped from that straitjacket. This is the only face I have, Dan. Whatever strange kind of life I find for myself, this is the face I take with me. I can never get another. But what can I do if – if even you cannot bear to look at me?'

There was a catch in her voice that was more dreadful than the scar. Dan made himself raise his fingers and touch her mutilated face. Made himself say, lightly, 'Don't be silly, Sal. What's a scar and a blind eye? Call yourself a pirate!'

'Oh Dan,' she said again. For an instant he thought she would cry. But instead she grinned and leaned forward to kiss him before she dropped the mask back into place.

Then she was gone, walking across the forecourt to take Francis's outstretched arm as he handed her into the coach. From the back, the two of them were the slender, stylish couple they had always been. Nothing had altered. Dan dug his nails into the palm of his hand and swallowed hard. He did not think he would be able to stand calmly and watch them leave.

Then, into his hand, slid Betty's rough fingers. She squeezed hard and whispered, 'Remember what Zachary said? Her's not done yet.'

The coach creaked into movement and Selina leaned through the window, her arm flourishing and her black mask flapping in the breeze.

'Just think,' she yelled defiantly. 'Think what letters *I* shall write you from Genoa!'

Standing shoulder to shoulder with Betty, Dan watched the coach draw away down the drive while Selina's arm sketched grandiose arabesques in the air.

* * *

142

At that very moment, across the Channel in Bayeux, a man in a brown coat set out from his lodgings to see if there were any letters for him. He was not pleased. Ellerby had been very slow to report on the second landing. Perhaps he needed a lesson. George's mouth curved unpleasantly as he strode along. Zachary was taken care of, at least. He knew nothing dangerous and a letter containing information about him was already on its way to the Exeter magistrates. That should put paid to Zachary for ever. Now he had served his purpose, he should swing, and nothing could save him. Most satisfactory.

That left only Francis. As he paced along the narrow street, George pondered the matter of Francis. It might be best for the family if he were allowed to escape. On the other hand, there was the small matter of Aunt Louisa's inheritance. . . .

Frowning with thought, he was just about to cross the street when a voice whispered from the alley behind him.

'Mr Merrowby.'

Automatically, he turned. Even while he moved, he remembered. He recognized that whispering voice. But by then it was too late.

Zachary was moving towards him out of the shadows, a triumphant smile curving his lips. And in his hand gleamed the long blade of his dagger.